HOLY

DETOX

Author ~ Taffie Beisecker

0

Endorsements

"This book is amazing and so needed today! As Taffie pours out her 'good, bad and ugly,' she reminds us of the hope that Jesus gives us to simply return back to Him. The bride is preparing herself without spot, wrinkle or blemish. 'Holy Detox' teaches us how to prepare ourselves to be the bride Jesus is longing for us to be."

Jeremy Lopez - Identity Network

"This book by Taffie Beisecker will engage your imagination to its highest degree. Not only is Taffie a personal friend, she is a prophetic friend as well. In this book, you will see what it takes to become the Bride of the Lord ... And the delivery of the word. She gives us nuggets of wisdom and a realism. I endorse this book and encourage all readers to submit to Holy Spirit and grow in the knowledge of GOD. Taffie's book will allow you to do that! GROW and Experience the living Word of the Lord."

Take A Leap of Faith into The Glory!

Dr. Theresa Phillips

Be A Part of The Web TV SHOW, GPVTV, www.GloryOils.com, DestinyArising.com, www.GlobalPropheticVoice.com, RedeemAndRenew.com

"In her new book, "Holy Detox," Taffie Beisecker writes on a subject that is dear to my heart, but in a fresh new way that kept me eagerly turning the pages. Her writing is unpretentious and easy to follow, yet she invites us to go deep into the greatest mystery of all time--the warm and welcoming presence of a God who actually waits for us to come and sit with Him. She made a statement that resonated with me, referring to the moment when she asked God if she could enter His presence whenever her heart desired. I absolutely love being able to go there when I want.

I appreciate being reminded that it's vital to use wisdom when getting into the secret place with God, realizing that He never calls us to do foolish things like neglecting our responsibilities or being lax regarding matters of godly integrity.

I especially enjoyed the section on dreams, some of them her own, and some from others, that so vividly demonstrate the depth of romance in the heart of God toward His beloved. Using great skill, she took it in a direction I've never seen before, even after reading many other books on the subject.

Through this book, I also discovered new and deeper meanings for the terms "covenant" and "surrender." I highly recommend this book if you are seeking a closer walk with the one who longs to know you best. You'll have to get a copy for your personal library if you are intrigued by the many ways the ancient Jewish wedding traditions parallel His loving relationship with His bride. As you read I guarantee that not only will you be educated and fascinated but also drawn into a deeper level of personal intimacy with Him.

And though we've all heard the scripture, "They shall know us by our love", her book reminds us that we may be the only gospel unbelievers will ever read, motivating us to prefer others to ourselves, in a new and deeper way, by the power of the Holy Spirit.

Her message may be a familiar one, but the insights there are fresh and new, and had me thinking, "Wow, what a powerful way to say that!" Now that it's a part of my library, I know I'll read its revelations again and again. I know you'll love it too, so run, don't walk for your copy of Holy Detox."

Steve Porter - Findrefuge.tv

Table of Contents

Table of Contents–cont'd

Foreword

"Within these pages, Taffie has given her intimate experience with the Holy Spirit and her passion for connecting with a desire for the presence of God. Each chapter will inspire you and breathe a new hunger to go deeper in your relationship with Jesus. It is a celebration of the gentleness and grace only discovered in a God-Centered life. Readers will be left drawn in, marked, touched and inspired that God's voice for their life will always be more than enough. It just may be another gentle whisper of the spirit saying "come closer and open your heart wider".

"Taffie's message within the pages goes a long way in providing necessary encouragement for anyone with the call of God upon their life. Like many anointed ministries over history, she now takes her place to provide a distinct message that our own faith and intimacy with the Holy Spirit will be expanded to believe that God also has a distinct plan and purpose for our life too. One that will not be diminished nor hindered by where we live, what might have been our circumstances or where we might find ourselves at this present moment. Rather, that in each of those moments in time God has been strengthening us and sensitively toning us to hear his voice. You will come away from reading her work with a new desire, encouragement and greater understanding of your destiny as a child of God.

I personally felt Taffie Beisecker helped me admit my need to silence the world around me and to rediscover the power *source of truth and unconditional love only found in the deepest communication with Christ. It reminded me that we really are a new breed of people in the spirit who need his touch to speak from the heart. You are in for an exciting read. You'll not be the same when you're finished."*

Sonia Genevieve Sherri
Neuropsychologist, Author, Speaker & Devoted Mother

Taffie Beisecker has been an ordained minister since 2005 and is the wife of Steve Beisecker. Between the two of them they have five grown children and one grandson, whom they are very proud of. Steve and Taffie are founders of The Threefold Cord LLC, an inspirational and prophetic ministry and an online blog, as well as a growing business.

Taffie is an author, speaker, and a minister of the prophetic. She carries a God-given passion for writing and a calling on her life to encourage, edify, equip and educate the Body of Christ, as well as people from all walks of life. Taffie ministers from the prophetic gift along with the knowledge, understanding and experiences she has been given opportunity from the Lord to receive and walk out in her own life.

She has a heart to;
**encourage the Body of Christ to be a people of love, genuinely as Christ loves us.
**encourage and educate the Body of Christ towards walking in true unity with one another.
**encourage every Believer in Christ to know and have a personal and intimate friendship with the Lord. Not only knowing Him as God and Father but also knowing Him as Friend.
**encourage ALL who belong to Jesus Christ to hear the voice of the Lord for themselves. Yes, EVERYONE! He's speaking, it's merely understanding how to hear Him.
**encourage every spirit-filled Believer to receive the total gift of salvation and to walk in the power and authority given to us by the Holy Spirit.
**encourage the Body of Christ to receive in their entirety, the gift of grace which has set everyone free from ALL bondage, (even from the

letter of the law of the old testament), and to not only receive it for yourselves but also recognize the same grace for those around you, as well.

*Many years ago, the Lord gave Taffie the mandate; **"As I tell it to you and teach it to you - you also, tell it to and teach others."** This book is a representation of that mandate in action.*

Intro

For many years, beginning more than a decade ago, I have had prophetic words spoken to me on many occasions about writing a book. Sometimes while speaking at, or simply attending a conference, people would approach me saying, "God told me to tell you, you're supposed to write a book." The confirmation was undoubtedly present but my response was always the same, "When He tells me what to write, I will do it." I would imagine I sounded much like a stuck record playing the same line over and over.

Oftentimes, we're waiting on the Lord to give us step by step, moment by moment, detailed foresight before we take the initial step into what we've already been told. We think we're waiting on God because, it's *not His timing yet*, while all along He's waiting on our obedience to take that first step out of the boat, in faith. It's safe to say, for each step we take in faith, it triggers the Lord to shine a light onto the next segment of the trail ahead of us.

For such a long time, I was waiting on the Lord to tell me what to write in a book while the entire time He was giving me prophetic words to speak, telling me what to teach at churches and conferences, and what to write in online published articles. Is this becoming clear to you much faster than what it did for me? He's been telling me all along what to write and patiently waiting on me to step up to the plate in obedience. It didn't come in the way I wanted it to, as in; hearing the title of a book being spoken to me and every word within its contents from start to finish - before I even made the attempt to sit down at the computer. In fact, as I sit here at my desk and type these words, I still do not have a clue as to what the title of this book will be. I tell you that, to let you know how unnecessary it is to know every detail of a vision from the Lord prior to launching out on it.

When it's time, He will deposit all we need to finish what He has instructed us to begin.

As I look back throughout my walk with the Lord, I now understand, for years He has been speaking to me what to write in this book beginning when He first commissioned me and gave me the mandate; *"As I tell it to you and teach it to you - you also, tell it to and teach others."* It seems so simple and obvious now. That is, *now* that I took that first step of faith.

There are many people who have come alongside of me for the creation of this book to be made possible. Above all is the Holy Spirit of course, to Whom all praise and credit is due. Obviously, without Him this book would never have existed. Secondly, my husband. He has prayed for me, supported me, encouraged and believed in me long before I ever came close to stepping out of the boat. He is certainly a gift from God and I am truly thankful I have been given the privilege of calling him my husband. Finally, my friends and intercessors who have so wonderfully spoken words of inspiration to me and have held shields around about me by way of their prayers and proclamations. They have without a doubt been a Godsend into my life.

Everything that I am sharing with you has come as a result from spending much time with the Lord in *the secret place.* One on One, intimate time with Him of worshiping, praying, listening and soaking in His Presence brings about such a sweet journey of revelation, meant to be shared. Within this book are revelatory insight and words that are precious to my heart. It leaves me somewhat feeling as if I'm allowing you to peek into the romantic notes from my Beloved. The word of the Lord is timeless. Although, some of the prophetic words in this book may have originally been released several years ago, it's possible you may find they speak to your heart now and into your present circumstances. If so, then receive them as encouragement and promises unto you from the Holy Spirit. God is not bound by time nor His word limited by time. His word is eternal and He *is* the Word.

"What you say goes, God, and stays as permanent as the heavens."
Psalm 119:89 (The Message)

Therefore, it is my prayer and hope that the contents of these pages will bless you, inspire you, cause your hunger for knowing the Lord to be stirred up for the first time, or even to be stirred up with a greater passion than what you've known previously. I sincerely pray you will find heart-felt hope, deeper understanding, greater clarity, and possibly some answers within these pages. Most of all, I desire that whatever the reason is for the Lord placing this book into your hands right now, *that* purpose will be fulfilled in its entirety.

"One thing I have desired of the Lord, That will I seek: That I may dwell in the house of the Lord all the days of my life, To behold the beauty of the Lord, And to inquire in His temple. For in the time of trouble He shall hide me in His pavilion, In the secret place of His tabernacle He shall hide me; He shall set me high upon a Rock." Psalm 27:4-5 (New King James Version)

Abundant Blessings!

Taffie

"My heart overflows with a good theme;
I address my psalm to the King.
My tongue is like the pen of a skillful writer."

Psalm 45:1 ~ Amplified Bible

CHAPTER 1

A Welcomed Intrusion?

I don't believe I will ever forget the reverential awe and the awakening within my spirit as I heard the Lord speak the words to me, *"Will you allow Me to be an intrusion into your life? Will you allow Me to intrude upon the time within your daily plans? May I come randomly at My will?"* Wow! When the Lord speaks to you, asking if He is welcomed into your life whenever He chooses to show up rather than when it's convenient, that's a humble awakening to say the least. He does not ask such a question without expecting an answer in response.

On first thought it seems it'd be easy to answer a resounding *'yes!'*. I mean after all, it is the God of the universe asking to visit. Quite honestly, to allow Him to intrude into our lives at any time He desires, at any time of the day or in the middle of the night - whether convenient or not, is not as easy to our flesh as one might think it to be. We become quite occupied in our schedules and daily routines and more selfish with our time than what we generally realize. Our agendas and to-do lists can oftentimes seem highly important to us, taking more presidency in our lives than what they ought to.

I responded to His invitation with a *'yes',* because the desire of my heart more than anything else was to have continual, intimate fellowship with the Holy Spirit. As deep as my love and desire for Him was, (and still is) I still had to learn a greater surrendering to Him than what I had ever understood. Sometimes, I would feel His presence so strongly while I was in the grocery store I felt as if I could barely continue to shop. At times, while on outings with other people He would beckon me into private fellowship with Him and I would excuse myself to the restroom for a few moments of prayer and worship. There were many times He would show up in the middle of the night while I slept, just to hang out with me for a bit. Admittedly, some of those times in the beginning, I found His middle of the night visits almost frustrating because my natural self wasn't yet disciplined. My flesh just wanted to sleep but He wanted to talk or was asking me to pray for someone. Those times of frustration didn't continue for long. As my natural-man became more and more disciplined to respond quickly to the beckoning of His Spirit, it became more and more of a delight to stow away with Him in the middle of the night. What began with feeling inconvenient soon turned into a wonderful eagerness for the next encounter.

I don't want to lead you into misunderstanding, when the Lord invites us into an incredibly intimate relationship with Him and He's asking to intrude into our lives wherever and whenever He wants, there *are* sacrifices we will need to make. There are adjustments we will need to make in our natural way of thinking. What we have perceived to be of our highest priorities within each twenty-four-hour period can no longer be placed in such an elevated position in our minds. If we keep the same perspective of priorities, we will find ourselves in a pattern of placing Him on the back burner. Even so, there's no need to be afraid His requests for time will come in such an absurd schedule it'll be impossible to submit to Him. Will it be inconvenient to our flesh at times? Yes, but not impossible. What I mean by that is - you might be thinking; *what if He asks me to stop and pray and it'll make me late for work?* or; *what if He wants my undivided focus when I need to be picking my child up from school?*

God is a good Father. He is wisdom. He is all about healthy balance and wanting the best for us. He will not demand you to stop and spend time with Him in such a way that it will cause you to lose your job or to be late in picking up your child. He loves people to walk in integrity; therefore, He will not cause you to compromise your integrity. In fact, He will not *demand* that you spend time with Him at all. He may beckon you lovingly but He will not be demanding and over-bearing. Spending time with Him will not take away from necessary time tending to your family or obligations of integrity.

He may wake you up in the middle of the night but I assure you, He will also restore your body as if being well-rested. He may ask you to pray before heading out to work but He will hear you and commune with you while you're getting ready or driving to work. He will teach you how to be in His presence in the most delightful and intimate way while at the grocery store, at the office, while driving down the road or tending to your children, while relaxing, working and certainly even while visiting with friends - anywhere and everywhere. It does not matter where you're at or what you're doing, you can always be in fellowship and in the Presence of the Holy Spirit as with one friend to another. He is fully aware of your circumstances and will meet with you in the best way possible as you make the efforts to meet with Him. Is it possible He might ask you to stay home from an outing you wanted to go to? Maybe, but if that's the case, you will by no means regret the time.

When you surrender your time back to Him, allowing Him in at all moments and hours of the day and night, you will discover your time has become enhanced. You'll be more alert and producing better results from your tasks at hand. The best part being, a non-stop communion and fellowship with the Holy Spirit, knowing Him as a person and no longer as merely an invisible symbol of God. It is impossible to meet with the Lord in such a way throughout your day and not soar to new heights in your relationship with Him. To me, it feels as if I've climbed aboard a spiritual rocket ship and lifted off from this earthly atmosphere. So, I'll forewarn you - be prepared for lift off!

Today, God is asking you the same question He proposed to me many years ago, *"Will you allow Me to be an intrusion into your life? Will you allow Me to intrude upon the time within your daily plans? May I come randomly at My will?"*

Maybe you've never known the type of relationship with the Lord of having a continual conversation and deep fellowship with Him; or maybe you at one time knew Him in that way, but need to return to a greater intimacy than what you are now experiencing. Whichever the case may be, He is anxiously awaiting you to open the door to His amazing invitation, which will be far more fulfilling than anything you've tasted as of yet. Once you have tasted of His sweet fellowship, you'll want more!

"Open your mouth and taste, open your eyes and see how good God is. Blessed are you who run to Him." Psalm 34:8 (The Message)

We are born into carnality *and* with a sure enemy, of which both plays its hand against God's truth to us. What does that mean in regard to this subject? Well, it means that as certain as you are reading this now, some will begin to hear thoughts like; *'that's for other people but not for me'*, or *'God doesn't want to fellowship with me in that way'*, or *'I've done too much wrong for the Lord to hang out with me. I'll wait until I get my life straightened out", "I have to work too many hours, I don't have time to set aside for God"*. Not one of those whispers you're hearing in your mind holds any truth to it.

I have three biological children and two step-daughters. All are very different from one another. My step-daughters didn't come to be a part of my family until they were grown so they have a slightly different perspective of my interaction as a parent with them. I did not raise them and tend to their needs growing up as I did my own biological children. Nevertheless, they are among my (grown) children now and I love them all with the heart of a parent. With that being stated, I did not include my stepdaughters into the following conversation for the reason being they weren't raised by me. Although in hindsight, their perspective on the subject matter would've been as equally interesting.

I found myself intrigued with this conversation that had taken place with one of my adult kids. I don't recall the specifics of how it began but I do remember that particular child mentioned something about - *it was obvious they had been my favorite while being raised.* I began to question why they thought *they* were my favorite child because, in truth, I had no favorite and yet each individual child was my favorite. We finished our discussion and it motivated me to inquire of my other two kids, asking if they also considered *that* child to have been my favorite. I spoke privately about this with each one, keeping all three unaware of my conversation with the other two. Fascinatingly enough, each one concluded they believed themselves to be my favorite child. And they were! Each one of them were my favorite!

A parent's heart is created to have as many *special* places in it for however many children they have. It enables each child to be the *'favorite'* in their own unique way, only they can be. God is our Father and His heart is the perfect heart of a perfect parent. We, on the other hand, as parents have our flaws and make plenty of mistakes along the way. Fortunately, God doesn't make any mistakes with us. He loves us perfectly and His every decision for us is perfect. Just as each one of our own children are our favorite, we also hold that very special place in our Father's heart that no one else except us, in our own unique individuality can fill. So, don't buy into the lies - YOU are His favorite and no matter what, He longs to spend time with YOU!

Regarding not having enough time left over to spend with the Lord after your work-day, it comes down to a matter of discipline and possibly setting aside something else to make room for Him. I worked a job that required working on most of the days of the week, coupled with long days of hard work. So, I understand the demand of time and the toll of physical weariness of such a job. I also understand that on most days we can choose to get up fifteen minutes earlier, make a point of using our driving time to pray instead of listening to the radio or instead of sitting in front of the TV in the evenings, turn it off and make a choice to spend time with the Lord in worship or in simple conversation about your day.

Not everyone has the luxury of an entire hour at a time - morning, noon and night - to give to the Lord but we do have the option of how we spend those few minutes in which we have in the morning, noon, and at night. The Lord isn't as much about quantity as what He is about quality and sincerity of the heart. There's quite a difference between someone who has a busy schedule due to parenting and providing an income for the household, as opposed to someone who withholds time from the Lord. Watching television, going out with the girls (or guys), playing on social media for example, does not describe someone who desires to make time with the Lord but is simply too busy. Rather, it describes someone who has many idols they are giving their time to.

It's quite possible that your friend can afford hours at a time to spend hanging out with the Lord, while you're working a full-time job and raising a family. The fifteen minutes you have available to set aside for Him is as valuable as what your friend's two hours are and will give you a return in your relationship with Him that is every bit as rewarding. He's not out to be the task master over your life, nor is He out to punish you for the time you cannot give to Him. He has His heart set on blessing you and rewarding every sincere effort you are making towards a relationship with Him. He isn't asking for the time you *don't have*. He's asking for what you're *withholding from Him*.

Recall the story of the poor widow's offering; *"Looking up, He saw the rich people putting their gifts into the treasury. And He saw a poor widow putting in two [a]small copper coins. He said, "Truly I say to you, this poor widow has put in [proportionally] more than all of them; for they all put in gifts from their abundance; but she out of her poverty put in all she had to live on." Luke 21:1-4*
(Amplified Bible)

Whether we want to believe it or not, sometimes we tend to have a quantity based mindset instead of a quality based mindset. By this I mean, we often believe having a greater quantity also means having a greater value. Quantity does not always reflect more when relating in terms of value. Take for instance, the value of one hundred pennies in comparison to the value of ten – twenty-dollar bills. Clearly, the pennies are of greater quantity but not value. This concept is also true when it comes to the value of words. Have you heard the phrase,

"They talked all day but said nothing at all"? Speaking many words does not necessarily mean you have spoken allot of valuable information.

If you give a person who is genuinely hungry a single bite of food, their stomach will not be filled nor will their appetite be satisfied. In fact, their hunger and desire for food will be aroused even more as the taste buds and digestive system becomes awakened and alerted to the presence of food. The human body's digestive system was designed to respond to that which is life sustaining and nourishment for it. You will soon discover that once you have tasted of communion with the Holy Spirit, your hunger for more will be aroused and you might find that you were starving for Him but not aware of it until you took the first bite. As spiritual beings, we are designed to respond to communion with the Holy Spirit much in the same way as our digestive system is to food. He is the spiritual nourishment (Bread of Life) to our spirit-man. Oftentimes, when a type of food we like is made available to us, we might tend to overstuff ourselves with it. Our enjoyment for it might send us into the 'can't get enough of it' mode. Likewise, we love it when the Lord speaks to us and fills us up with lengthy conversation and much direction in a variety of areas. When we begin to experience this, we may find we cannot get enough of hearing from the Lord. We cry out for *more, more, more Lord*! He, of course delights in our hunger and our desire for His fellowship with us. Nevertheless, He does not always choose to speak to us in lengthy conversations. Sometimes He chooses to say allot in only a few words. It's important that we realize, even the most valuable, life-changing information and conversations may be found within merely a few words. Just as the wisdom of our natural fathers can be conveyed to us at times in only a small amount of spoken words, so it is also with our Father God. If you find yourself waiting in His Presence and becoming disappointed in hearing only a few words from Him be assured of this; He is delighting in your fellowship and much depth can be expressed in only a minimal amount of words. Let's not forget how few and yet how powerful are the words, *"It is finished"*.

"The one thing I want from God, the thing I seek most of all, is the privilege of meditating in his Temple, living in his presence every day of my life, delighting in his incomparable perfections and glory."

Psalm 27:4~Living Bible

CHAPTER 2

The Prodigal Brides Are Returning

Oftentimes the Lord will speak to us through dreams to convey specific insight that we otherwise may not have revelation of. Just as God speaks to each of us uniquely while we are awake, He also speaks uniquely to each of us while we are sleeping.

Dreams can sometimes be difficult to understand, given many times they are filled with people and things which are symbolic for something else. The meaning of what you're viewing in the dream may be totally different than what it's symbolizing. On the contrary, not all dreams are filled with such symbolism, some are made easy to understand, being their meaning is exactly as dreamed.

If you're like me, there have been many occasions of struggling with trying to understand the meaning and significance of a dream. There have been several times God gave me a dream in which I had absolutely no doubt it originated from Him and yet I could not understand it. There can be so many varied factors involved with why we may not perceive or understand the meanings of our dreams. Among the list of contributing factors, in my experience, there are a few that stands out above the rest.

First off, in our natural reasoning we might be trying too hard to figure out the 'symbolisms' in the dream. When that's the case, we might be looking past the obvious, making it more complicated than need be.

It's also possible that we're stumbling all around the revelation of the dream because God may desire us to function together as the

22

Body, in an *'every joint supplying'* effort. He would therefore choose to give one person the dream and another the interpretation. This keeps us in a humble place of understanding how we truly do need one another's portions. Personally, I have found when this is the case, the Lord will give me a persistent prodding to share it with a specific person.

I believe one of the most common reasons we have the greatest struggle with dream interpretation is because we've been given the dream ahead of its 'appointed - *revelatory* time'. I am not going to even try to pretend that I may know or understand God's reasons for doing what He does - He IS God and I am NOT! With that being cleared up (wink); There are times He does give us insight (albeit, partial insight) for some of His decisions. I tend to ask the Lord, 'Why?", quite often. Sometimes He will give me an answer and other times He tells me it's not for me to know and I am only to trust Him in His ways, without an explanation'. A few of the *"why's?"* I have asked over the years have been, *"Lord, why did You give me this dream so far ahead of its time?"* or *"Why did You give me this dream but not tell me its meaning?"* The reasons can vary greatly and I have learned along the years I cannot take one answer and apply it to every dream. There certainly must be Holy Spirit led discernment with each individual dream. Then again, there *can* be a general guideline followed if we're careful not to lock it into a hard-fast rule, preventing the Holy Spirit the liberty to speak differently to us in future times.

Why would God give us a dream before its appointed time to be revealed? It's the same reason why He may speak vaguely or give a glimpse to us about our future. He knows us too well and knows we may become too eager to fulfill the things He has shown us. We might become anxious and run ahead of Him being determined to make happen what we have been shown. When we do that, we are bringing what we saw in the dream into existence by our own strength and in our own timing instead of God's – and *that's* a formula for disaster!

You might be asking, *'why even show us at all before the appointed time?'* Here's the answer the Lord gave to me when I asked that same question; When we have a dream even if we do not have the revelation of it at the time, things begin to take place within our spirit. A seed of revelation begins to develop deep within us, possibly without realizing it's happening. You see, our spirit grabs ahold of spiritual seeds much like when we pray in our spiritual language. In our spiritual prayer language, we don't have the interpretation of it most of the time but our spirit discerns the unknown language from our heart and it's a perfect prayer that cannot be tampered with nor sabotaged by our own logic. Likewise, we may be given a dream months or even years ahead of its time of manifestation, with no interpretation or understanding. When the appointed time arrives, it's most likely we'll then discover how much equipping has been taking place within us from the time of the dream to the time of its fruition.

"For the revelation awaits an appointed time; it speaks of the end and will not prove false. Though it lingers, wait for it; it will certainly come and will not delay." Habakkuk 2:3 (NIV)

Later, when we are given the revelation of the dream we're then able to grasp it from a much deeper place of understanding than when it was first given. Often, by the time we receive the understanding we may also have the surrounding circumstances lining up with the dream (or at least at the brink of it). Waiting on the revelation from the Lord in its appointed timing ensures us to not misinterpret our dreams into wrong circumstances or twist and stretch them, making them fit into our present time - prematurely.

The funny thing with dreams is, we may spend a long time trying to understand them and when the unveiling comes, their interpretation seems so obvious! That's why it's called, *"revelation"*. Revelation means; *"act of revealing; the disclosing to others of what was before unknown to them; that which is revealed; often, a striking disclosure."*

I've had dreams that I have literally waited *years* to receive the revelation about. Once I had the understanding, I felt as if I must have been impaired to not have known the meaning of them previously. Their meaning seemed as clear and as obvious as the nose on my face. The fact is, in a way I was *impaired* from receiving the interpretation until the appointed time was to arrive. It's as if God was saying, *'I'll give her this undisclosed foresight to get the seed planted on the inside of her, then let's wait it out until the perfect time to tell her anything further, lest she gets the plan all messed up.'* That may be ad-libbing a bit on how His delivery might be (smile) but it paints the picture.

There may be times the Lord will give us dreams meant for us only, as a personal insight. Other times, the dreams He gives to us are for insight extending to the Body of Christ.

One of the ways God gives me the discernment of whether a dream is only for my personal insight versus for the Body of Christ is how I appear in the dream. If I am merely a spectator in the dream or if my appearance is not as I truly am, then I know this is not a dream intended for only myself. For instance, in a dream of this nature I may have the appearance of a man, a child, or possibly a female that does not carry any resemblance to me whatsoever.

The following is an example of such a dream:

I was a young woman, perhaps within the age range of early to mid-twenties. I was involved in a relationship with a young man who had proposed marriage to me. Although it was not yet official with a wedding date, there seemed to be a peace and a trust in the solidity of the relationship. This young man was muscular and very handsome. He was also genuinely a good person and trustworthy. He was fun, interesting and someone you just knew walked in integrity, and one whom you could always count on to follow through with his word. I felt very passionate about him in my heart. As I thought about our future together, I knew he would provide a lovely home and be intentional in providing all that I would need. I sensed it would be an enjoyable life, having more than just basic needs met, but not lavishly pursuing material abundance. The joy we would have together would come more from the pleasures of life itself.

Although I was in a definite relationship with this young man, somehow, I'm not sure how it came about, but I began to take up company with another young man. It was more of a social relationship. Whenever we were together in one another's company we were never alone. Our time spent together was always in public places. This man would be considered as, 'a nice person', yet his character didn't seem to quite match up to the other young man's. There was a lack of depth with him that was present with the first man. Physically, he could be described as an average-looking person. There was nothing in his personality, nor his appearance that would cause him to stand out above the rest, unlike the other man. What did stand out though, was this man had great wealth. His family owned their own business, which was very prosperous and thriving. He was very generous with his money and when making a purchase, he spared no expense. Often, after being in his company, I would later find a bundle of money he had secretly placed inside of my pocket. This man also proposed to me. After the proposal, he took me to his home to show me how lovely it was, and all that I would have access to if I were to marry him. His great wealth most assuredly was showcased in his house. If it were not the 'finest of the finest', he did not want it in his house. He was very meticulous, wanting everything to be in its proper place, always in order and organized and very predictable.

The dream ended as I was telling the second man's sister, the decision I was faced with. I had to make a choice. I realized, both men could not stay in my life, and whichever one I chose, the other would have to go. I awoke knowing who it was that I truly loved.
(The first young man!)

The young woman in the dream represents the Church, the betrothed Bride of Christ. The first young man; the one that stood out above the crowd in his good looks and character, represents the Holy Spirit. He is everything that has real, true purpose. Nothing about him or within him reflects anything to be considered superficial. In Him is depth and strength. He is beautiful to behold. The second young man had knowledge of the relationship and the commitment between the woman and the first man and yet still sought to entice the woman in becoming his bride. He offered her what could appeal to her flesh but nothing that had lasting value. This man represents the traditions of religion. Everything that is being shown and offered is nothing of a true relationship but is only what makes you temporarily feel good. The time spent together was only represented in public places because there was no place of intimacy, which is needed for a true relationship. Good friends become so dear to one another because they have taken the time for intimate conversation, getting to know one another's heart.

In this dream, the Lord is revealing to us - His Church, we are at the crossroads of decision. This is a personal choice and decision each one of us will individually face.

Daily, spending time in the Lord's presence; in His word, in worship, sharing your heart in conversation with Him and listening to Him share His heart with you, (aka; prayer) establishes true intimacy and friendship with Him. It can best be described as a *sacred romance* and it's in this type of relationship with Him, you will find the liberty of the Spirit and know Him for who He *really* is. Knowing Him defies what man's doctrine depicts who He is and the beliefs within it of how you must present yourself when approaching Him.

The decision we all must face? To resist or to agree with the temptation to turn away from our *"First Love"* and fall back into the entrapment of the doctrine of religion. The danger and the snare of religion is, it's not always as easy to detect as one might think. Most of the time, we become ensnared because we step into it with the most well-meaning of intentions. Don't misunderstand me, I totally support the function the local churches have for *the* Church. We're not to forsake the assembly of ourselves and I believe it to be very vital for the edification, fellowship and joint supply of the Body of Christ.

On the flip side, there can be a difference between what the Lord has called us to do as the Church and what we, or someone else may have called us to do. At times, what He has called us to and what the local church has called us to are one in the same. The danger comes at the times when there's a difference between the two. When we have become overly focused on performance within the local church we have then become about *religion* rather than, *the Church*. It can be very easy to spend all our time and energy attending or tending to the various kinds of programs and activities within our local church. In our busyness of doing all that we think is necessary sometimes before we realize what has happened, we have busied ourselves *away* from the first-love-relationship with our Savior because He did not *fit* into our schedule of required duties. We get so busy *doing* everything we think is about Him that we no longer have time *for* Him. If we become preoccupied with *duties* and forget the relationship with the Lord within our time at church or in our daily walk, we then have nothing more than a religion, a program or a daily routine that does not stand out in a crowd above the rest.

With the second fellow, there was social time spent but no real time with depth or intimacy included or being established. The time was only superficial. The reward in the relationship was only temporal, nothing being offered had eternal (lasting) value. If you were to take away all the material possessions he had, there was nothing left that made him stand out from any other man.

If you were to take away all the material possessions from the first man, he still had everything that fueled the passion of the heart because what made him stand out from the rest came from internally. It's who he was. From the perspective of him representing the Spirit of God, Who He was, is "I AM". He IS our all in all. Within Him is everything we could ever think of, need, desire or hope for.

A relationship with our Lord isn't simply knowing about Him. Neither is it in fulfilling duties within our local church. It's daily interaction with Him. It's a fiery passion that burns within the depths of your heart for Him and from that posture you can recognize His presence within you. Yes, true intimacy is within all of what I just mentioned and so much more! It's a relationship and not a religion because you know Him and He knows you.

"Do not store up for yourselves [material] treasures on earth, where moth and rust destroy, and where thieves break in and steal. But store up for yourselves treasures in heaven, where neither moth nor rust destroys, and where thieves do not break in and steal; for where your treasure is, there your heart [your wishes, your desires; that on which your life centers] will be also".
Matthew 6:19-21 (Amplified Bible)

Recently the Lord spoke to me, *"The prodigals will come home when they are no longer being enabled"*. Implementing the word 'prodigal' as a *noun* it can be defined as such; *1: one who spends or gives lavishly and foolishly; or, 2: one who has returned after an absence (Merriam-Webster).*

This could take into consideration as a prodigal being a person who is not merely spending lavishly in terms of money and resources but also to include the careless spending of; time, talents and possibly even our callings (casting our pearls before swine, perhaps). It also may include a parting away from; our first love, the use of our gifts and talents, a calling, a physical household, or possibly a departure from specific convictions of a lifestyle.

Using these definitions as our guidelines there are many of us in the Body of Christ who could therefore, at some point within our lifetime be considered as a type of prodigal in one way or another.

Enable - (Merriam-Webster): to make (someone or something) able to do or to be something: to make (something) possible, practical, or easy.

God said, *'the prodigals will come home when they are no longer being enabled'.* Have we unknowingly been enablers? It's time that we do a thorough accountability check to evaluate whether we are (out of good intentions) potentially enabling the very ones we are praying for. It was by no coincidence this word was spoken to me the day before an opportunity arose for me to be an enabler within my own life. It may be more accurate to say, for me *to continue* to be an enabler. The Lord allowed me to see the very action I thought was being helpful and compassionate was instead, harmful. It was enabling someone to continue down a dead-end path rather than becoming awakened to a better and more beneficial way for them. The growth they needed would require them to go through some growing pains which is never easy to walk through nor is it easy to watch someone dear to you walking through it. Even so, the truth remains, sometimes growing pains are a necessary part of acquiring maturity and a healthy lifestyle.

Not only should we do a thorough check of how we might be enabling others but from time to time also do a deep heart check of how we might be enabling ourselves to continue a path that is not beneficial. What excuses have we been telling ourselves? What have we been blaming someone else for when the true accountability lies right here at our own doorstep?

There's no condemnation to be found here. In fact, it's quite the opposite. It's a call from the Holy Spirit to step up into our full potential He has placed within us. It is also an opportunity to ensure we're not hindering those around us from walking in their full potential, as well. Our good intentions to help take care of others can sometimes prevent them from a step in the learning process they need to go higher. There are instances when our intervention can be a stumbling block as opposed to the stepping stone our good intentions wanted it to be. There's freedom that comes with realizing we've been enabling ourselves and maybe even someone else. Once the revelation is made known to us it allows us to reach a higher altitude for vision and advancement in our lives.

A few days prior to the Lord speaking this word to me about the prodigals, I had a dream. It was similar to the dream of choosing between the man of the Holy Spirit and the man of religion, with a slight variation of meaning.

I dreamed; *a good friend of mine was involved with dating two different men at the same time. These two men were very different from one another in pretty much every aspect. One man was much more attractive to the natural eye, as well as having an outgoing personality that was full of energy and charisma. It seemed that whenever she was with him, it was an enjoyable time, filled with nothing but fun. Everything was about being recklessly carefree. There really wasn't much of anything that had to do with getting to know one another on a personal level or anything of depth. Nor was he a man of commitment to anything, or to anyone.*

The other man she was dating was slightly older, not such a heart throb in appearance or personality. He wasn't reckless in his spending, or in the way he carried out fun activities, nor was he someone who made decisions on a whim without thought of consequence. He was a man of integrity, stability, depth, security, true to his word, genuine in his love and commitments, he had a peaceful strength about him that emanated security. He was a faithful provider who was filled with wisdom, yet in no way a fuddy-dud who didn't enjoy having fun within the positive adventures of life.

My friend was caught up in the circumstances of enjoying the dating relationships of both men. She was passionately drawn to the more reckless man, due to a desire for the thrill of adventure, which gave her an escape from the mundane, everyday lifestyle. At the same time, she deeply desired security and commitment, of which she knew he would never offer, nor could provide because it was not within his heart to do so.

The other man, with the peaceful strength about him, deeply loved my friend and desired to marry her. Not going along with the usual traditions in asking for her hand in marriage, he instead, chose to do a surprise wedding for her in the same way as one might arrange a surprise birthday party. He contacted her friends and family members to help strategically take her to the venue on the correct date and ensure she was dressed in the wedding dress he provided for her, at the correct time. We were also requested to be there to witness this event as those who loved her and wanted nothing more than for her to be blessed.

The day of the surprise wedding came and we were all there. Just as planned, my friend was there in her wedding dress. Without question, she wore the dress. The reckless man was there, wearing a well-tailored suit and positioned at the entrance as an Usher. He directed the guests to their seats and the unknowing 'bride to be', down the aisle. She proceeded to walk down the aisle, still having no clue of the destiny awaiting her at the end. I watched with such joy as my friend so beautifully walked toward her groom.

When she arrived at the altar, her groom greeted her by placing on her finger, the symbol of his commitment to her. In the same moment as she said, "yes" to her groom, they entered an instantaneous marriage covenant. There was no lag time between the acceptance of his proposal and the covenant being established.

As the dream was ending I could feel her heart was fulfilled with everything she longed for, but had not previously realized it would ALL be found within the relationship of this one man alone.

This dream can be viewed as a sort of parable for insight into the process that many people struggle with in coming into a relationship – *fully* with Jesus Christ. How often it is we start out wanting a relationship with Him but unwilling to give up the seductions of the world. (When speaking of the seductions of the world, I'm not categorizing it in only sexual seductions. The world's seductions can be many things. Anything that might lure our focus and draw us away from Christ and walking in His calling is a seduction of the world.) They're everywhere and so tempting to fall into their traps. The seductions of the world are within movies, songs, product advertisements, clothing, sports, career promotions, social media, you name it. Almost anything and everything within society has a seductive lure, fishing to draw us in. When the world's seductions have become the commonplace of society from our workplaces to our entertainment choices, even within the advertising of our foods, the temptation to join in can become overwhelming and seduce us into taking the lure every now and then. Before we know it, we've taken the bait and find ourselves dating both - the world and the Lord - without a genuine commitment to either one.

In this dream the bride is symbolic of those in the Body who are being tempted by the seductions of the world. The momentary thrills that have no life-giving capabilities and their outcome results in a draining away of the higher perspective. The Holy Spirit is the Groom. The groom was presented as initially not being physically attractive because much of the time when people consider living as a Believer, at first glance the lifestyle doesn't appear alluring. It's not until taking the step of commitment with Christ, the fulfilment is then discovered and you know He is everything you've been looking for. The friends and family assisting the groom in the surprise wedding represent those who are praying diligently for their *prodigal* friends and relatives to enter back into what the Lord has for them. Although the prayers of these people may be in secret and not seeming to show much signs of fruit initially, their prayers are effectively powerful and will prove to be in due season.

My friend put the dress on without question because she was being adorned with what had been created for her from the time she was in her mother's womb. She was created to wear this bridal gown and it had been created to become her covering, adorning her to identify as the Bride to Whom she belonged. When we step into that which we have been created for and likewise was created for us, it becomes a part of our being. It is connected and woven into the very fiber of our identity and we find a greater sense of completion, knowing who we truly are. We were created for a covenant relationship with God through Jesus Christ.

"Let us be glad and rejoice and give Him glory, for the marriage of the Lamb has come, and His wife has made herself ready. And to her it was granted to be arrayed in fine linen, clean and bright, for the fine linen is the righteous acts of the saints." Revelation 19:7-8 (New King James Version)

I asked the Lord as to why I saw the reckless man at the wedding and positioned at the entrance as an Usher. He gave me understanding that in our covenant with the Lord, life is not void of adventure and thrill as our carnal minds would have us to believe. In fact, as we enter our walk with the Lord in the fullness He has beckoned us into, adventure awaits us - in its *refined* form (that is, without the presence and the quest of superficial and temporary gratification). It greets and escorts us along the way in the direction we are called to go in. It simply does not carry the same recklessness and lack of discernment in what is satisfying as opposed to the empty thrills the world points us toward. In other words, what we perceived as adventurous and thrilling in the scope of the world's viewpoint takes on an entirely new appearance in the presence of the Lord's refinement. It transforms to an adventure with lasting pleasures and eternal rewards.

We are created to find our fulfillment from the covenant relationship with our Creator. It's how we were designed, and so it is the only way we will ever find true lasting contentment and become completely satisfied. If we have not entered covenant with Him we find ourselves on a continuous journey to fill the void within us. This is likened to feeding the natural stomach. You eat but the food does not provide a lasting solution. In a short amount of time you're hungry again and must eat often to satisfy the demand of the stomach.

Any attempts we make to fill this hunger with anything other than relationship with the Father are merely temporal solutions and will not come close in comparison with what the longings of the heart is yearning for. The instant gratification the world offers only leaves us with a bigger void and a frustration for the lack of finding what *hits the spot*.

The Lord is sending out an invitation to each one of us in this season to return to Him, to go deeper with Him or possibly come to Him for the first time ever. His desire for us is to enter a relationship with Him with all of who we are and to walk in our full calling in Him.

We are standing at the entrance of a season or *time,* if you will, of this present generation soon to be unprecedented to any time before this. We are a people who are called not only to preach the word of the Lord with our voices but also to preach it through demonstration. Miracles, healings, deliverance of demonic bondage, raising the dead who have gone prematurely, salvation being received by those who are considered the least likely people to receive salvation - are merely a hint of what we are called to be manifesting and are at the verge of seeing and experiencing.

The Lord is delivering to us a great beckoning to walk away from ALL that is hindering us from stepping into the fullness of relationship and destiny He has marked us for. He desires us to be awakened to His kingdom within us and reject the temptations from the world's draw that lead us nowhere beneficial.

In the dream my friend was unaware that the man of integrity was everything she ever wanted until she fully gave to herself to him exclusively. Only the Lord can provide us with all we have been searching for, and more. When we entrust Him with who we are and all that we have, nothing is ever squandered.

This is an amazing time to be alive! He is an amazing Father calling us back to Him in such a loving way, with a rewarding destiny - desiring that we not miss out (or squander) on anything He has intended for us in such a time as this. This is a time of awakening and celebration-for the prodigals are returning home.

"All things are lawful [that is, morally legitimate, permissible], but not all things are beneficial or advantageous. All things are lawful, but not all things are constructive [to character] and edifying [to spiritual life]. Let no one seek [only] his own good, but [also] that of the other person."

1 Corinthians 10:23-24~Amplified Bible

CHAPTER 3

Here Comes the Bride!

I heard the Lord speak to me; *"Who are the true worshipers? This is the question of today that I ask, and yet do you know the answer? Oh, My love, My Bride – the one whom I adore, you are so precious in My sight. I have made it so simple for you. For those who worship in Spirit and in Truth are those worshiping Me as My Bride. They are those who come to Me in love and not by means of an extended hand with motives of seeking My treasures for selfish gain. It is not My will that you should substitute a relationship with Me, with My treasures. I want your heart, your whole heart, not a portion that I must compete with another god in your life.*

Faithfulness. I pour out My river of living water upon those who are thirsty and call out My name, and on those who answer the call when they hear My voice, I will cause to drip with an everlasting oil.

My Bride, I beckon you with My very life and I impart My life into you. Listen to My heart. My heart speaks to you of My love. This is a love affair that I am having with My Church, My Bride. For those who worship in Spirit and in Truth are those worshiping Me as My Bride. Do not fear or be hesitant of testifying of this crazy, passionate love, because this is the love the world is seeking for and yet does not find. I love you, My Church, My Beloved – with the most fragrant love and with the purest kisses of My Spirit. Holy Bride, I adorn you in My beauty, in My peace, in My love, and in My grace. This is a love letter to you, My Beloved!"

Immediately after the Lord finished speaking this to me, I had a vision of a scroll on the ceiling. I saw the scroll roll back and the open sky was revealed. Through the opening a white horse descended. The Holy Spirit told me, *"This is the Spirit of Revelation"*.

Whenever I have written or taught about being the Bride of Christ, I normally get a big response. However, the responses vary from those who are excited about the topic to opposition from those who believe Israel is the *only* Bride.

"For your Creator, will be your husband. The Lord Almighty is His name; He is your Redeemer, the Holy One of Israel, the God of all the earth." Isaiah 54:5 (Living Bible)

For God to be Israel's husband means there was a covenant established between them. Of which, He did through Abraham and all his descendants. When the Lord establishes a covenant, it is meant to be everlasting, until death causes it to be severed. A covenant is an agreement between parties that binds them together within an established legal contract. Marriage is such a covenant between husband and wife.

In the natural it would be defiling to the marriage covenant for a spouse to give their affections of the heart to another person outside of the marriage. It's just as equally defiling for someone who is in covenant with the Lord to turn their affections to another, albeit; a job, a person, money and even a ministry. In the natural, to partake in thoughts of the heart or outward actions with another person is considered adultery, as is also anything that pulls our affections from the Lord to something else is spiritual adultery.

In explanation, when you worship the Lord you are offering and surrendering your heart and adoration to Him. Worship is a time of communion with the Holy Spirit that *releases* to Him and *receives* from Him. You are releasing your heart and vulnerability to Him during worship as well as receiving His presence (Spirit) and therefore His transforming power *into* you. It's very intimate because it's all about the heart.

"These people honor me with their lips, but their hearts are far from me. Their worship of me is pointless, because their teachings are rules made by humans." Matthew 15:8-9 (GOD'S WORD Translation)

The definition of worship is as follows: *reverence offered a divine being or supernatural power; also: an act of expressing such reverence; a form of religious practice with its creed and ritual; extravagant respect or admiration for or devotion to an object of esteem (Merriam Webster)*

Wherever we put the abundance of our attention will eventually be where the adoration of our heart is also. We were created to transform into the likeness of that which we worship *because* we were created to worship God. If we worship money, we become all about materialism. If we worship religion, we become religious. If we worship fame, we become prideful. If we worship God, we become vessels of love.

Yes, God *is* married to Israel. But the story does not stop there. His bride - Israel, began to worship other idols. *Because of* His unconditional love and everlasting covenant He established with His bride, the Lord beckoned Israel to return to being His faithful bride and offered complete forgiveness to her.

"Again, I ask, "Didn't Israel understand that message?" Moses was the first to say, "I will make you jealous of people who are not a nation. I will make you angry about a nation that doesn't understand." Isaiah said very boldly, "I was found by those who weren't looking for me. I was revealed to those who weren't asking for me· Then Isaiah said about Israel, "All day long I have stretched out my hands to disobedient and rebellious people." Romans 10:19-21 (GOD'S WORD Translation)

"So, I ask, "Has Israel stumbled so badly that it can't get up again?" That's unthinkable! By Israel's failure, salvation has come to people who are not Jewish to make the Jewish people jealous." Romans 11:11 (GOD'S WORD Translation)

"But some of the olive branches have been broken off, and you, a wild olive branch, have been grafted in their place. You get your nourishment from the roots of the olive tree. So, don't brag about being better than the other branches. If you brag, remember that you don't support the root, the root supports you."
Romans 11:17-18 (GOD'S WORD Translation)

Although God's original covenant was with Israel only, His new and lasting covenant is now with *ALL* of us through Jesus Christ. Research in genealogy shows the graph of the so-called 'family tree' as having many branches extending from various levels of the tree. All of which are connected and come from the same root. Likewise, we - His people, are grafted-in branches extending from the same root therefore sharing in the same inheritance as what the original branches of the Olive Tree does. Jews and Gentiles are now both grafted in as one, in Him. Therefore, we are all His Bride!

In the modern-day western culture, our process of marriage goes something like this; we see a significant other of whom we are attracted to – we then begin dating. We fall in love. We become engaged and on an agreed upon date we go through a somewhat short wedding ceremony by exchanging vows with one another and signing some legal paperwork. *WAAHLAAH!* We're married and off onto our honeymoon.

In an Ancient Jewish wedding the process was slightly different. Keep in mind, the scriptures were written during the times of ancient Jewish weddings. The wedding was performed in two stages. The first stage was the *Betrothal* and the second stage was the *Consummation*. Betrothed means to engage or promise in marriage by a mutual consent. In other words, the betrothal is an agreed upon contract. Consummation means to carry to the utmost extent or degree, or to bring to completion. Which would make it the last step that completely seals the contract.

Let's discuss the betrothal stage of the marriage process. Being betrothed to one another is somewhat like being engaged to one

41

another. Although, there is a difference in how our culture considers engagement to be. Our present-day idea of engagement is basically to assure the other person of our commitment to them. During the engagement, we are not yet at that time making a legally binding agreement or a consolidation of our possessions, so to speak. It's more of a promise for a *future* event.

On the other hand, an ancient Jewish betrothal was a binding legal contract and was recognized in their society as if already married. It was quite possible for the betrothal process to take an average time of twelve months to complete. To break the betrothal, a certificate of divorce had to be given.

I would like to give you a comparison of how the Lord grafted us in with Israel, making both Jew and Gentile His bride. I'll do this through laying out the steps of the New Covenant alongside the ancient Jewish wedding ceremony.

Ancient Jewish Wedding: The first step in the wedding process comes when the man who is ready to take a wife chooses the woman he wants for his bride. Once he chooses her, he then must receive his father's blessing for the marriage process to begin. To do that he invites the woman to his father's house. She knows the customs of the culture and understands when this takes place, she has the choice to accept his invitation or to reject it.

New Covenant: *"You didn't choose me! I chose you! I appointed you to go and produce lovely fruit always, so that no matter what you ask for from the Father, using my name, he will give it to you."* John 15:16 (Living Bible) ~ Jesus chose us.

Ancient Jewish Wedding: If the woman accepts the invitation, she then enters the father's house to meet with the father and his son. The father, son and the bride all know this is the first stage in the wedding process and is to be taken seriously.

New Covenant: "Look, I'm standing at the door and knocking. If anyone listens to my voice and opens the door, I'll come in and we'll eat together. Revelation 3:20" (GOD'S WORD Translation) ~ Whoever accepts Jesus' invitation will be taken to dine with Him.

Ancient Jewish Wedding: The father and son will at that time present a marriage contract to the bride. Within this contract are promises that the son makes to the bride, telling her what he will do for her within their marriage covenant.

New Covenant: "God's divine power has given us everything we need for life and for godliness. This power was given to us through knowledge of the one who called us by his own glory and integrity. Through his glory and integrity, he has given us his promises that are of the highest value. Through these promises you will share in the divine nature because you have escaped the corruption that sinful desires cause in the world." 2 Peter 1:3-4 (GOD'S WORD Translation) ~ Jesus has told us we will share in His divine nature, as a part of being in covenant with Him.

Ancient Jewish Wedding: The contract also states what the bride's obligations are within the marriage covenant.

New Covenant: "But because the God who called you is holy, you must be holy in every aspect of your life." 1 Peter 1:15 (GOD'S WORD Translation) ~ We, the Church must present ourselves as holy to fulfill our obligation to Christ.

Ancient Jewish Wedding: A price is listed of what the man is willing to pay for his bride.

New Covenant: "You were bought for a price. So, bring glory to God in the way you use your body." 1 Corinthians 6:20 (GOD'S WORD Translation) ~ Jesus bought us with the price of His life and blood.

Ancient Jewish Wedding: The man and woman drinks a sip of wine from the cup to seal the contract of marriage. Both drinking from the cup signifies they have now become one and they both know the marriage contract has at that point been made official and is legally binding.

New Covenant: "When supper was over, he did the same with the cup. He said, "This cup that is poured out for you is the new promise made with my blood." Luke 22:20 (GOD'S WORD Translation)

The disciples were very acquainted with the wedding ceremony traditions and marriage covenant so they understood very well when they drank from the cup they were becoming *as one* with Jesus. Thus, all He had would become theirs' also.

Ancient Jewish Wedding: The father and son give gifts to the bride as proof the marriage contract was sealed. This was evidence that could be seen by others, proving there was indeed a binding marital contract.

New Covenant: "However, Christ has given each of us special abilities—whatever he wants us to have out of his rich storehouse of gifts. The psalmist tells about this, for he says that when Christ returned triumphantly to heaven after his resurrection and victory over Satan, he gave generous gifts to men." Ephesians 4:7-8 (Living Bible)

"In addition, he has put his seal of ownership on us and has given us the Spirit as his guarantee." 2 Corinthians 1:22 (GOD'S WORD Translation)

~ He told us He would not leave us alone with nothing of His, so He gave us the gift of His Holy Spirit to indwell us until He returns for us.

Ancient Jewish Wedding: The bride would place a veil upon her face that all could see and know she was set apart for her husband only. She now belongs to him and to him only. No one else is allowed to look upon her because she is a married woman. Even though they have not yet consummated the marriage, they are considered legally married. They have taken the vows and she is to walk in purity, reserving herself for her husband.

New Covenant: "But if you give yourself to the Lord, you and Christ are joined together as one person." 1 Corinthians 6:17 (Living Bible) ~ Although we are not yet living with Christ, we are recognized in all the spirit realm as being His Bride, therefore we conduct ourselves in acknowledgement as being His.

Ancient Jewish Wedding: It is now when the husband and wife will part ways for a time. The husband will go away with his father to prepare a bridal chamber for his bride in his father's house. As they depart from one another, the son would say to his bride something like; *'I go prepare a place for you and when my father tells me it is ready, I will come and receive you unto me.'* During this time, the husband and bride will not actually be together. She has the promise of the gifts to take with her, ensuring her he will return for her when the preparation of the bridal chamber is complete.

New Covenant: "My Father's house has many rooms. If that were not true, would I have told you that I'm going to prepare a place for you? If I go to prepare a place for you, I will come again. Then I will bring you into my presence so that you will be where I am. You know the way to the place where I am going." John 14:2-4 (GOD'S WORD Translation)

Ancient Jewish Wedding: It is the father's responsibility to tell the son when the chamber is complete and the time is right to go receive his bride. The son does not know when the father will decide it's time. Only the father knows.

New Covenant: "No one knows when that day or hour will come. Even the angels in heaven and the Son don't know. Only the Father knows." Matthew 24:36 (GOD'S WORD Translation)

Ancient Jewish Wedding: The next step is the consummation process. Just prior to consummation the bride would disrobe, dip down into a pool of water to signify she is clean and sanctified for her husband.

New Covenant: "He did this to make the church holy by cleansing it, washing it using water along with spoken words. Then he could present it to himself as a glorious church, without any kind of stain or wrinkle—holy and without faults." Ephesians 5:26-27 (GOD'S WORD Translation)

Ancient Jewish Wedding: Because the father is the one who appoints the time for the son to return for his bride it was common for the bridegroom to return in secret, suddenly and unannounced prior to his arrival. Oftentimes, he would arrive late at night.

New Covenant: "Therefore, you too, must be ready because the Son of Man will return when you least expect him." Matthew 24:44 (GOD'S WORD Translation)

Both: Once the Bridegroom receives His bride unto Him, He will then bring her to the marriage supper!

The Church was birthed two-thousand years ago, but she - the true Church - has been hidden away for the most part. She's been trying to understand who she is, if you will. It's in this generation that the Church is coming of age and is about to be 'revealed' as who she really is – the glorious Bride of Christ. The *'awkward, unsure of who she is'* stage is about to be done away with. The Bride will shine forth, knowing who she has been created to be. The glory of her Groom shall shine brightly upon her and all who see her unveiled face (who she has been transformed into) will know Who it is that she belongs to. It is His seal – the covenant seal of His Holy Spirit which is the evidence and the radiance she is adorned with.

The betrothal stage of the wedding of the Church took place while Jesus was on the earth. That's when this marriage contract was made legal. For that very reason, we can walk in the same power and authority of Christ because we have been given His name and in *all* the spiritual realm it is recognized as a legal and binding contract.

Let's talk about our relationship with the Lord, as His bride. How often is it that we approach Him in timidity? Are we unsure that He wants us to get close and intimate with Him?

A husband delights in his bride approaching him. He desires the intimate fellowship with her that is only between the two of them. In the same manner, our Holy Bridegroom delights in us approaching Him confident in knowing He wants our fellowship. He welcomes us into a rich and deeply personal, intimate relationship. He wants us to know Him as a husband and wife know one another within the marriage bed. That may seem way out there to you, but it's nonetheless true.

"On that day, she will call me her husband," declares the Lord. "She will no longer call me her master." Hosea 2:16

"Israel, I will make you my wife forever. I will be honest and faithful to you. I will show you my love and compassion. I will be true to you, my wife, then you will know the Lord." Hosea 2:19-20 (GOD'S WORD Translation)

The word "know" in this scripture in its original Hebrew meaning is the same as what is used in *Genesis 4:1 "And Adam knew Eve as his wife, and she became pregnant and bore Cain; and she said, I have gotten and gained a man with the help of the Lord."*
(Amplified Bible – Classic)

"Then Adam had sexual intercourse with Eve his wife, and she conceived and gave birth to a son, Cain (meaning "I have created"). For, as she said, "With God's help, I have created a man!" Genesis 4:1 (Living Bible)

The original translations of the words 'know' and 'knew' in these scriptures is describing the sexually intimate relationship of a husband and wife in marriage. If the Lord is telling His people of Israel that His will is for them to 'know' Him, He is talking to them about having a relationship with Him which is deeply intimate and within the covenant of marriage. (I want to clarify – so no one gets all weirded out and thinking I'm referring to some cultish practices. I don't mean a physical sense of intimacy whatsoever. This is strictly in terms of the spiritual relationship within the heart -being as one.)

Spiritually speaking, we can have that deep, intimate relationship with our Lord. He created us to know Him in a fellowship of communion. We should not fear approaching Him in transparency. He wants us to fellowship with Him just as we are. He wants us to know His heart because we have gone near enough to hear His heartbeat. Here's the thing, it's impossible to know someone, I mean really know them up-close and personal, unless you spend quality time with them. Knowing *about* someone because of what you have been told is not the same as getting to know who they are from the interaction *you have directly with them.*

Now that you know, we are His Bride, don't go back to the former way of knowing Him – from afar. Get up-close and personal with Him. Remember, He created you for Him – for His eyes – for His pleasure, for His heart, for Him knowing you and calling you by His name. He sees you as the most beautiful creation there is. When the Holy Spirit beckons you, answer Him with confidence, knowing fully well He is delighted and willing to hear your prayers, to talk to you, or to sit quietly with you because He enjoys your fellowship and receives your worship whole-heartedly.

I would like to encourage you to make it your purpose to get to know the Lord more today than you did yesterday, and more tomorrow than what you do today.

"He took some bread and gave thanks to God for it. Then he broke it in pieces and gave it to the disciples, saying, "This is my body, which is given for you. Do this in remembrance of me." After supper, he took another cup of wine and said, "This cup is the new covenant between God and his people— an agreement confirmed with my blood, which is poured out as a sacrifice for you."
Luke 22:19-20~NLT

CHAPTER 4

The Seed of the Holy Spirit Births Good Fruit

Approximately two thousand years ago, the Church was birthed and is now coming of age and ready to give birth. *WHAT* is the Church birthing? The glory of the Lord displayed as '*His Kingdom Come*'!

The Holy Spirit told me He is, "*purifying His Church and there is a separation coming that will reach into the entire world. It's a separation of what has been birthed out of the flesh from what is birthed out of the Spirit of God. Many ministries, projects and churches who have been self-appointed will suddenly step down as the purifying begins. Those who have been commissioned by God to be His anointed leaders, called to carry His presence, will not be allowed to keep alive anything that has been birthed out of the flesh. God is calling forth a Bride that is pure, without spot or blemish. A Bride that conceives and gives birth to only what is of her Husband's Seed and not of another.*"

When saying, '*birthed out of the flesh*,' that would be about anything that is not of the Holy Spirit. Religion comes from man's way of traditions and mindsets, therefore, someone who has been called by the Lord but has been led by the ways of religion rather than the Holy Spirit, would fall into this category. Please understand, He is not removing them (at least not permanently) rather, He is washing off what is not of Him.

Within the perfect will of God, when the marriage is consummated there is an exchange of blood. This blood exchange is a *blood covenant* that has taken place between the bride and groom. It's a covenant that God recognizes as existing for a lifetime. When we receive Jesus as Savior, we are partaking of the Blood of Jesus and in so doing, we are partaking in a marriage covenant with Him, as His Bride. It is also a covenant recognized by God, with the difference being - it does not *end* upon death from this life, on the contrary, it continues throughout eternity.

Prior to the new covenant with Jesus we were married to the law. Since God recognizes covenants as a lifelong binding agreement, the way to be released from a marriage covenant by His plan of design, is for one of the two people to exit by way of death. Likewise, to be released from the law (the law was the first covenant with man) there had to be death. Jesus came as God dwelling among us, embodied in flesh just as we are, and fulfilled the law on our behalf, releasing us from it through His death. The word says, when we were baptized into Christ Jesus we were also baptized into His death. As being buried with Him, we were also spiritually resurrected with Him into a newness of life. The old man passed away and we became a new creation. Thus, allowing us to be released from the former covenant/marriage to the law, (by being partakers in His death) into a new covenant/marriage with grace – now being transformed as the Bride of Christ.

"If you have died with Christ to the elementary principles of the world, why, as if you were still living in the world, do you submit to rules and regulations, such as, "Do not handle [this], do not taste [that], do not [even] touch!"? (these things all perish with use)—in accordance with the commandments and teachings of men. These practices indeed have the appearance [that popularly passes as that] of wisdom in self-made religion and mock humility and severe treatment of the body (asceticism), but are of no value against sinful indulgence [because they do not honor God]." Colossians 2:20-23
(Amplified Bible)

The keeping of religious traditions or of legalistic doctrines and regulations (Jesus calls them *"commandments of men"*) is conceived and birthed of the flesh. A false mindset, believing there is a need to perform by *works* to receive or maintain righteousness is the root of motivation behind this so-called doctrine of beliefs. This mindset yokes a person into bondage with the spirit of religion and opposes the Word of God, which declares liberty by grace.

We are made the righteousness of God in Christ Jesus through grace and *"not by works, lest any man should boast" (Ephesians 2:9)* By the Spirit of God we have been set at liberty from the law. Trying to keep the law is bondage. Once we have been made free from the bondage through salvation, we are only under the bondage of the law again if we go back and place ourselves under it.

"But the child of the slave woman was born according to the flesh and had an ordinary birth, while the son of the free woman was born in fulfillment of the promise. Now these facts are about to be used [by me] as an allegory [that is, I will illustrate by using them]: for these women, can represent two covenants: one [covenant originated] from Mount Sinai [where the Law was given] that bears children [destined] for slavery; she is Hagar. Now Hagar is (represents) Mount Sinai in Arabia and she corresponds to the present Jerusalem, for she is in slavery with her children. But the Jerusalem above [that is, the way of faith, represented by Sarah] is free; she is our mother." Galatians 4:23-26

"But what does the Scripture say? "Cast out the bondwoman [Hagar] and her son [Ishmael], For never shall the son of the bondwoman be heir and share the inheritance with the son of the free woman. "So then, believers, we [who are born again—reborn from above—spiritually transformed, renewed, and set apart for His purpose] are not children of a slave woman [the natural], but of the free woman [the supernatural]." Galatians 4:30-31 (Amplified Bible)

You cannot live in the perfect law of liberty, which is grace, *and* strive to keep *some* of the law. If so, you've denied the sufficiency of grace and are bound to keep the entire law. If we continue to go back to the old covenant law we are being driven back to the old mindset by the religious spirit, and are not walking towards the goal of being the pure, spotless Bride of Christ.

It was for this freedom that Christ set us free [completely liberating us]; therefore, keep standing firm and do not be subject again to a yoke of slavery [which you once removed]. Galatians 5:1

You have been severed from Christ, if you seek to be justified [that is, declared free of the guilt of sin and its penalty, and placed in right standing with God] through the Law; you have fallen from grace [for you have lost your grasp on God's unmerited favor and blessing]. Galatians 5:4 (Amplified Bible)

David was the anointed leader of God. He was chosen by the Lord to be king among the people – God's anointed. If you recall in 2 Samuel, chapters 11-12, David and Bathsheba committed adultery from which they gave birth to a son. David's son is symbolic of what was conceived and birthed from the desire of the flesh, which is sinful in its own nature.

In James 1:14-15, the word says this about the desire of the flesh; *"But each one is tempted when he is drawn away by his own desire and enticed. Then, when desire has conceived, it gives birth to sin; and sin, when it's full grown, brings forth death."*

Flesh gives birth to sin, and in sin is the seed of death. The seed symbolizes the spirit. The spirit of sin brings death, but the Spirit of holiness, which is the Holy Spirit, brings life.

"Live in me, and I will live in you. A branch cannot produce any fruit by itself. It must stay attached to the vine. In the same way, you cannot produce fruit unless you live in me. "I am the vine. You are the branches. Those who live in me while I live in them will produce a lot of fruit. But you can't produce anything without me."
John 15:4-5 (GOD'S WORD Translation)

Whatever you are rooted in determines the kind of fruit you will produce. If you're a branch on a vine, you produce the same type of fruit of that vine. It is impossible to produce a fruit different from the vine you are attached to and growing from.

In Matthew 7:17-20, Jesus says; *"Even so, every good tree bears good fruit, but a bad tree bears bad fruit. A good tree cannot bear bad fruit, nor can a bad tree bear good fruit. Every tree that does not bear good fruit is cut down and thrown into the fire. Therefore, by their fruits you will know them."* In other words, you can know the type of tree that the fruit came from without ever seeing the tree itself, just by discerning what the fruit is. I can hold in my hand an apple and know without a doubt that it came from an apple tree, even though I never saw the tree with my own eyes. A snake is born from a snake, a bird is born from a bird. We produce our own kind. If the fruit is corrupt, then the seed is corrupt, as well as the tree because the fruit did not produce itself; it is a product of the tree from which it came.

Throughout history, there have been many people come and go who are speaking and doing things they say are in the name of the Lord but have been far from His will. Some of these people have influenced and swayed many from the truth of the word of God. For this reason, plus many more, it is necessary that we abide in Jesus. It is in the place of abiding in Him, we will know Him intimately enough to quickly discern when an imposter comes along, deceitfully posing in His name. When we draw near to God in such a fellowship of intimacy, we are abiding in the presence of His Spirit, and in the presence of the Holy Spirit there is perfect liberty.

"You will know the truth, and the truth will set you free."
John 8:32 (Living Bible)

"So, if the Son sets you free, you will be absolutely free."
John 8:36 (GOD'S WORD Translation)

Regulations, traditions, commandments of men, and religious doctrines all fall into the same category – bondage. For as many who are searching for any of those to give them a sense of being a 'good' person and free from sin, the truth to be told is, they do not – will not - and cannot – ever make us free. The Son of the *Most High* makes us free. In Him only, are we made free. Within the rules and regulations of man-made doctrine and religion, there is no place for liberty and very little allowance for grace. In the pursuit of trying to perform and keep the statutes of those doctrines, a person becomes yoked with that religion.

"I know that you're Abraham's descendants. However, you want to kill me because you don't like what I'm saying. What I'm saying is what I have seen in my Father's presence. But you do what you've heard from your father." The Jews replied to Jesus, "Abraham is our father." Jesus told them, "If you were Abraham's children, you would do what Abraham did. I am a man who has told you the truth that I heard from God. But now you want to kill me. Abraham wouldn't have done that. You're doing what your father does." The Jews said to Jesus, "We're not illegitimate children. God is our only Father." Jesus told them, "If God were your Father, you would love me. After all, I'm here, and I came from God. I didn't come on my own. Instead, God sent me. Why don't you understand the language I use? Is it because you can't understand the words I use? You come from your father, the devil, and you desire to do what your father wants you to do. The devil was a murderer from the beginning. He has never been truthful. He doesn't know what the truth is. Whenever he tells a lie, he's doing what comes naturally to him. He's a liar and the father of lies."
John 8:37-44 (GOD'S WORD Translation)

In this scripture, you can see that with their words they claimed to be rooted in God, but in discerning the identity of their fruit, they proved to be rooted elsewhere. Everything on the outside had the appearance as being from God. They did many religious acts and even in their speech they were proclaiming to be of God. The keeping of legalistic traditions prevents the liberty of the Holy Spirit from being free to move among us and through us. When examining the root of why legalistic traditions are enforced, it seems to take us back to the same reasons the Pharisees were wanting to kill the very Word of God. The root from which they grow opposes the root of that which produces the fruit of the Holy Spirit.

God wants our whole heart given to Him. Why? Because if our entire heart is not set on Him, then some portion of our heart must be given to something else. Which means, there is an opening made for flesh to conceive and give birth to what is not from God.

Yes, we have seen along the years some of the Church stray away, conceive and birth what was of the flesh and yet proclaim it to be of God. He is holy, therefore we are to be holy and are to pursue holiness by way of receiving His grace in faith, NOT by works. That's where many have become confused; trying to work their way into holiness. It is not possible. We cannot allow flesh-made doctrines to remain among us. In the surrendering to Him and turning away from what we once thought was the pursuit of holiness, we *will* encounter different areas of the Holy Spirit that have not been so familiar to us. That's alright, there's so much to who God is, we will never be able to experience every facet of Him while still in these earthen bodies. As for that matter, I'm not positive we will be able to experience every facet of Him throughout all eternity!

With each passing day, I find myself more and more grateful for the grace that is poured out to me through Jesus. Grace is a gift which was born from the seed of Love. We didn't pay for it, nor did we work for it. It cannot be earned or else it would no longer be a gift, but rather, a wage. As freely as it was given to us, just as freely should we be issuing it to those around us. None of us *deserve* it, but all of us need it.

David was a man after God's own heart because he humbled himself and repented of his sin. Forgiveness abounds through grace. David did not continue to walk in the consequence of his sin with Bathsheba. When he repented, he was free from the bondage of that sin, therefore submitting to the will of God, which brings forth life and blessings. David and Bathsheba, later gave birth to another son, Solomon, whose wisdom and understanding was multiplied greater than any other man's. That's what the face of redemption looks like through grace. When the sin was gone, it was gone completely. There was no longer a need for bearing the heaviness of it, for it did not exist after it had been cleared. Blessing existed thereafter.

I would like to say that I have no place of religion found within me. That is simply not the case. I have come to understand that those of us who have been raised in a religious-indoctrinated church atmosphere from the time of childhood, for the most part, we walk through the process of detoxing from religion. I may think that I'm totally clean from it, but then when I look back from where I am now to where I was five years ago, I see the growth. Understanding that the five years prior to that, I was much farther along than what I was five years before that as well. Nevertheless, as I become less and less religious, (works, law, not agreeing with condemnation) the more and more I like myself. Why? Keeping ourselves bound into a system of rules and laws is a surety for failure. In that system, we have no choice but to continuously focus on our shortcomings. On the other hand, "grace", freely given for us to freely receive, sets us into the liberty of relationship that we may focus upon God's love and blessings for us.

God is NOT religious! Isn't that the best news you've heard all day? I am so thankful He is not the condemning god, ready to thump us at any given moment, the way religion wants us to believe He is. He's not our condemner waiting for us to mess up. He certainly wouldn't have to wait very long, if that were the case. None of us would have a hope of lasting more than a few minutes before we were "thumped". The truth is, He truly loves us and His desire for us is to give us *life more abundantly*. His heart is to bless us and surround us with edification, because that extends from His love. Don't get me wrong, He's a good Father, so yes, He does correct us because that's what good father's do when they love their children. It's called teaching, and it's easy to receive and brings us a greater freedom, unlike the condemnation of religion which is a heavy weight upon us.

When our Father looks upon us, He sees the finished, mature, complete person He has created us to be. That's His focus on us, not the flaws that we see with our natural perspective, those are merely temporal. He sees from the perspective of eternity.

A while ago, the Holy Spirit spoke to me saying, *"There is a separation now beginning. A separation of the sheep from the goats. (Matthew 25:32-33) There are herdsmen who have been trying to drive My sheep in the wrong direction. The herdsmen are unclean spirits, imposters of the truth. The herdsmen are those spirits that are the driving force behind those who have the appearance of godliness but deny the power. (2 Timothy 3:5) The power of godliness is the transforming power of the Holy Spirit which is able to transform the heart and renew the mind."*

God is raising up the worshipers in these last days. *"But a time is coming and is already here when the true worshipers will worship the Father in spirit [from the heart, the inner self] and in truth; for the Father seeks such people to be His worshipers. God is spirit [the Source of life, yet invisible to mankind], and those who worship Him must worship in spirit and truth." John 4:23-24 (Amplified Bible)*

The appearance of worship without the active participation of the heart is only vain religion. I heard the Lord say, *"As My Spirit of Truth moves upon you, cutting off the apostasy of the flesh, receive of the fresh revelation that My Spirit brings, which is the manna that you shall be fed daily. Do not run away because of what seems strange to you, for this is My truth and My beckoning."*

Religious mindsets have been one of the biggest bondages the Church has struggled with. Religion tells us we cannot simply be who we are, that we'll never be good enough as we are. It delivers the message that we must look, speak, and do everything a certain way, or else who we are, what we say, and what we do isn't acceptable. Religion turns us all into clones rather than having the freedom to be the unique individuals we were created to be.

The Lord has given us this time of awakening to clearly see the bondages that have held us captive. They may be different for each one of us, and yet some may be quite similar. As we learn to become aware and awakened to what we have already been given the freedom from and therefore need to cease in going back to, we are moving from glory to glory in the true liberty of His Spirit. So, Church, let's be excited and do our happy dance, knowing we are His anointed and are about to birth what is of Him – fruit that is full of life, drenched in His love, total liberty, bearing His likeness and HIS NAME!

When we try to keep rules, even when it's unspoken rules, believing we must all speak, act, and look the same as everyone else, then we are striving to keep man's traditions and it's a form of religious works. Striving to keep the form of religious works is a stronghold of the mind, and keeps people in bondage. An affair with the law or religion only produces offspring of bondage to sin. Rather, our faithfulness to;

"the Holy Spirit produces this kind of fruit in our lives: love, joy, peace, patience, kindness, goodness, faithfulness, gentleness, and self-control. There is no law against these things" Galatians 5:22-23~New Living Translation

CHAPTER 5

Is "Christianese" the Language of God?

Currently there are so many ways of expressing ourselves through diverse types of communication. If you give it much thought at all, it's almost mind boggling of all the avenues modern technology provides for us to connect with one another. We can communicate faster, and in a greater variety of ways than ever before. It's nearly unimaginable how easy technology has made it for us.

Just the other day we needed some assistance with the programming of our computer and the IT person who corrected the issues did so remotely, from his office in India. That's amazing to me. Technology even has the capability to translate one language to another, making it possible for us to communicate with one another, whereas we'd otherwise have a language barrier. What an amazing time of communication we are blessed to live in.

Communication varies from; speaking to one another face to face, letters in the mail, texting, phone calls, social media, emails, photos, body language, gestures, symbols, and much more that I'm likely to be unaware of. It's amazing! And yet, with all the advancements in communications through technology, we still cannot adequately translate into words nor discern another individual's personal, unique thoughts and beliefs, found only within the heart. No amount of technology can compare with being able to directly communicate person to person - heart to heart.

I have found through experiences of my own, there are some matters of discussion best to be had when the capability to hear one another's tone of voice is available. Hearing the tone of voice seems to leave a much smaller gap for misinterpretation of the conversation at hand.

Obviously, communication is highly important in every aspect of life. Whether it be between employer and employee, the leaders of countries, teacher and students, or on the level of two people in a personal relationship, proper communication is a must. Without proper communication, there can be no understanding for; the task at hand, the instilling of education, unity, or even the ability to peaceably agree to disagree. Ensuring proper communication is necessary for us to get onto one another's level of understanding as much as possible.

In other words, if you speak English and you're speaking to someone who does not understand English, it benefits neither one of you to continuously try to have a conversation solely in the English language without another means of interpretation. There comes a point when you must find a way to translate your words into the words that pierce the other person's understanding. Otherwise, there's a void without a bridge by which to connect. This seems a simple enough concept to understand. If so, then why do we oh-so-often expect everyone else to understand what we believe and know, at the level we now believe and know it at? Plus, the entire time we're trying to communicate with those other people, we're using a type of language per se', we may not have even started out understanding. I have been there – guilty as charged.

I have realized at times in the past, I had the frame of mind - if I think and perceive a specific way, then everyone else also thinks and processes information in the same way as I do. Do you know what that's called? Being in the box - even when it seems to be a good, or a godly (in appearance) way of expression.

Within the same language there can also be variances in how we speak that language. Take for instance, slang. Slang is a derivative of the language we speak, yet it can be different enough that it becomes difficult to completely understand if you've not been privy to it. I used to work in a facility where there were many employees much younger than myself and their primary language was that of slang. Although they were speaking English as I do, at times I could barely understand what they were saying. I thought, how can we be speaking the same language and at the same time I feel as if I'm listening to a foreign language? No exaggeration.

As Spirit-filled Believers, our manner of speech oftentimes is a good example of being in the box and expecting everyone else to be in the same box with us. We, as Believers, often seem to have a common language by which we speak to one another with. Much of how we relate to one another is in connection with the understanding of our faith, beliefs of God, and knowledge of scripture. If you recall in the beginning of learning scripture and about the Lord, most of what we were hearing and reading seemed almost like a foreign language. I can only speak for myself, but my understanding of all those things did not take place overnight. It was over time. In fact, many years into it, I'm still learning and coming into a better understanding. My point is, so much of the time we're speaking to people on the level of understanding and beliefs that we have, expecting them to receive it all as we do currently. On top of that, we expect them to receive it with the same gladness we have about it. The reality is, a person cannot receive anything, (let alone with gladness) of what they don't comprehend due to a language barrier.

We seem to want the other person to get on our level of communication, don't we? Maybe we are the ones who need to be a little more considerate of the other person and learn to communicate in the language they best understand.

"That is what is meant by the Scriptures which say that no mere man has ever seen, heard, or even imagined what wonderful things God has ready for those who love the Lord. But we know about these things because God has sent his Spirit to tell us, and his Spirit searches out and shows us all of God's deepest secrets. No one can really know what anyone else is thinking or what he is really like except that person himself. And no one can know God's thoughts except God's own Spirit. And God

has actually given us his Spirit (not the world's spirit) to tell us about the wonderful free gifts of grace and blessing that God has given us. In telling you about these gifts we have even used the very words given to us by the Holy Spirit, not words that we as men might choose. So, we use the Holy Spirit's words to explain the Holy Spirit's facts. But the man who isn't a Christian can't understand and can't accept these thoughts from God, which the Holy Spirit teaches us. They sound foolish to him because only those who have the Holy Spirit within them can understand what the Holy Spirit means. Others just can't take it in." 1 Corinthians 2:9-14 (Living Bible)

There is no doubt in my heart and mind, God's word is truth. Nor is there any doubt for me that His very word of truth is what sets people free. Here's where I bring this long-winded explanation full circle; the truth of His word does not merely emerge in the form of quoted scripture. This is where we-Believers have gotten into a religious form of speech, thinking we are only speaking God's word if it's done in the form of exact scriptural word usage.

There are those people who can receive scripture spoken from the *New King James* language, with understanding. On the other hand, there are those who can receive the very same truth when it is spoken from our common language we use every day in ordinary conversations. God's truth is God's truth, period. It does not lose power to transform a heart and mind just because it was in words other than direct quotes using chapter and verse when being said.

We can quote John 3:16, or we can as an alternative explain to the person, God's love is way bigger than anything we have done and He loves us so much He sent His son to take our punishments for us. He is always willing to forgive whatever it is we've done wrong in our life, if we will simply believe that Jesus is His Son and took the due punishment in our place.

Jesus was not a bible thumper. I mean no offense by this terminology, but He was much more considerate of people than that because His main concern was about the person's heart rather than their grammar. He got on their level of communication, which is why the *New Testament* is full of Him speaking parables. His parables were stories the people could relate to, and for those who had a heart to understand they could through these types of teachings. Scripture used in the wrong timing can turn out to be like a weapon of condemnation rather than God's intended purpose of lifting, setting free and bringing hope and salvation. There is a right time and place for everything and that does include scripture quoting. Jesus spoke one way to the religious leaders of His time, He spoke another way to His disciples and those who had understanding, and then He spoke yet a different way to those who weren't religious nor understood the Spirit. To them, He spoke using parables about the common daily life of the people in their generation. Those analogies were what most of the people listening could relate to.

Doctors have a greater knowledge of the functions and systems of the human body than what the average person does. They're not born with this knowledge of course, they spend years studying and being taught through written information, as well as, hands-on experience before they graduate to a well-informed and professional level. Therefore, the terms and language skills they use among their peers is vastly different than what they use when speaking to those of us who are uneducated in the medical field. Thankfully so! Otherwise, what would we understand of their diagnosis to us? Zilch! Knowing that, they bring their explanations down to our level of understanding that we may be able to relate to what they are informing us of. I can understand it much more clearly if my doctor tells me I have the common cold rather than if he says his diagnosis is that I have *nasopharyngitis, or rhino pharyngitis*, or even *acute coryza.*

Although we eat our healthy portions of solid foods every day, a newborn baby doesn't come into the world eating solid food. It's not that it wouldn't want it if it had a taste of it, or even that it refuses to eat it, rather, it's not equipped to eat it because it's young digestive system hasn't been developed enough to handle it. What may be good and nutritional for us as adults, would be quite harmful to an infant. The bible often refers to God's word for salvation and grace as milk, and the more in-depth scriptures as meat. If you consider it in that aspect, the newborn baby analogy can be compared to those who do not yet understand God's word and His ways. As the infant grows and develops more-so, *little by little* it becomes more capable of expanding its diet and will begin to desire a greater variety of foods when it's more matured digestive system can then safely handle them.

Whether we're in a position that we have little-to-no understanding of scripture or not, somewhere in life we all can connect to a common place in something. We're all people and all share the fact that we have been given life here on earth. We all know joy, pain, trials, successes and so on, and somewhere in those commonalities we can connect on some level. Whether infant or elderly, native or foreigner, male or female, Christian or Muslim, educated or uneducated, there is one language that reaches into the heart better than all others. That is, how we treat one another. God's language. Love in action. Love never fails.

The moral of this chapter is, we've been speaking 'Christianese' far too long and the rest of the world cannot understand the language we speak. Goodness, sometimes I can't understand the language we speak. It's time to come out of our religious boxes. Some of us may need to get off our religious soap boxes, (I say that with nothing but love) and start speaking the language that we can all relate to as normal people who live in this world alongside everyone else. Let's replace our 'Christianese' language for 'People-ease', shall we?

"Saying the right thing at the right time is like a golden apple in a silver setting."
Proverbs 25:11~ERV

CHAPTER 6

Becoming Love in Action

It is the most valuable gift you can give or receive. It cannot be purchased, although some have made attempts to. It cannot be fabricated, nor can it be given at all without the presence of sincerity. If you receive it from another, treasure it, hold it dear to your heart and consider it precious. It is priceless, beautiful and the most sought after treasure. It's had movies, songs and books written about it. People have even given up their lives for it. What is it? .... LOVE!

So, body of Believers, where is the love? It's not found in the good works done before man for public applause. It's not in the judgment we all so quickly pass on one another. It's not in the leaving our fellow man to endure trials and burdens all alone. It's not in the backbiting and gossipy lips that ruin another's reputation. BUT! It is in the being kind to one another, in the standing with your fellow man through their hardships and struggles, it's in the patience we give to one another in our growth process, in the understanding that none of us deserves grace more than any other therefore allowing grace and mercy to abound above all else. So then tell me, where is the love? For LOVE is the greatest gift of all. God IS love. If you live by the Spirit of God, then you live by the code of love. Continuously in our responses and decisions, we should be asking ourselves two questions; What does Love (God) look like? What would Love do?

"God loved the world this way: He gave his only Son so that everyone who believes in him will not die but will have eternal life. God sent his Son into the world, not to condemn the world, but to save the world."
John 3:16-17 (GOD'S WORD Translation)

God is calling us back to the foundation that our very faith and salvation was established on. It's the true message of the Gospel – it's the pure testimony of Jesus Christ. We've built a lot of structures upon the foundation, but now it's time to tear them down and get back to the indisputable truth among the denominations and the Church in general, finding that place of unity with whomever it's possible. Although we're being taken back to ground one, it's not a message for lack of maturity, it's a message containing more power than what you can imagine!

If Jesus came so the world might find salvation through Him, and His Spirit now dwells in us, as the saying goes; *'The Jesus in us may very well be the only Jesus the world sees, until we point the way to Him.'* Therefore, shouldn't the world be able to find a form of their salvation through us? Don't misunderstand, I'm not saying *we* are the door or the entrance of any sort of way, Jesus is the *only* Door. I am saying, as Ambassadors of Christ, we are representatives of Him and should be carrying the same essence as who He is.

The Greek word for 'salvation' is, *soterion (so-tay-ree-on)* and it means; *rescue, deliverance, safety, and health. It covers the total man; spirit, soul and body.* (heart, mind & physical being)

We - born again, spirit-filled Believers, have been given the truth, the power of the Word and the Spirit to; rescue, bring deliverance, provide safety and the provision of good health, by one means or another – to all people – first of our own household of faith, and then to the world. All of which covers; spirit, soul and body.

"Dear brothers, what's the use of saying that you have faith and are Christians if you aren't proving it by helping others? Will that kind of faith save anyone? If you have a friend who is in need of food and clothing, and you say to him, "Well, good-bye and God bless you; stay warm and eat hearty," and then don't give him clothes or food, what good does that do? So, you see, it isn't enough just to have faith. You must also do good to prove that you have it. Faith that doesn't show itself by good works is no faith at

all—it is dead and useless. But someone may well argue, "You say the way to God is by faith alone, plus nothing; well, I say that good works are important too, for without good works you can't prove whether you have faith or not; but anyone can see that I have faith by the way I act." James 2:14-18 (Living Bible)

We are to put action to our faith-talk in order that we might take care of the whole person, rather than only their spirit. Without action to back it up the faith we speak of is null and void. I believe just as *action* is a necessity to prove faith exists, it is just as necessary to put action to our love-talk, as well. If we say we love one another, but there are no actions to prove that love, as; *'faith without works is dead'* – then love – which is greater than faith, creates a greater void without the works to give it life.

There are three types of love referred to in the bible. The first one I'll mention is the Hebrew word *"Ahab"* (ah-hahv). *Ahab* means; *to have affection for; romantically or, as a friend.* – it's a general word for *love* that covers a range of varieties of love. With this word description of love, it is so general it could be regarding; you love the food on your plate, you love going for walks, your dog, your friend or your significant other. It's very general.

The second type of love comes from the Greek word, *'phileo'* (fil-eh-o) and it is used for; *a friend; or having affection for someone; a matter of sentiment or feeling; as in to kiss, or love.* With this type, there is a personal attachment involved. *Ahab* and *Phileo* love deal more-so with *emotions*, and can be easily subject to change.

The third type of love comes from the Greek word, *Agape (Ag-ah-pay)*, which means; *love, affection or benevolence; a love feast; charity, dear, love.* The definition per Webster's Dictionary of "benevolence" is – *the disposition to do good; good will; kindness; charitableness; the love of mankind, accompanied with a desire to promote their happiness. An act of kindness; good done; charity given.* Unlike the other two types of love, agape is much more of involving the *will* and upon a *decision.* It entails an unconditional love because it's with intention to endure.

It's the love that gives up self for another, it's the love that will endure beyond all else. I personally believe, unless agape love is the foundation for every type of love then it will not have what it needs to endure the storms, maintaining an everlasting love.

If we're being real, relationships can get messy. Real life and real love aren't scripted out for us as we see it depicted on the Big Screen. Being the imperfect people we are, living in imperfect conditions and situations, things can get quite messy while we're still figuring out our walk of love. The bright side is, while we don't have a Hollywood script written out for our lives, we do have a script of sorts, written by the Creator of love Himself. As imperfect as we are, it's more than just a *possibility* for us to love with a perfect love because God is love. If God is love and His Spirit inhabits us, so does His perfect love. Therefore, through Him we can love with the same type of Love He loves us with. Not because we make no mistakes in loving one another. On the contrary, we make plenty of mistakes, but grace is powerful enough to cover each one if we allow it. Being conduits of His love flowing through us, we can love and love well.

There is safety in mature love. It's not easily offended, it does not judge or at the very least - not quick to judge, it prefers and chooses to see the best in others, it builds up with the intent to strengthen the other person – even amid them falling short. God is love and where the Spirit of the Lord is; there is liberty to be transparent in who we are because there is no fear in perfect love. Whether it be friendship or beyond, the deepest and lasting relationships are without a doubt the ones that can express their thoughts and hearts to one another. Safely. The friend who is not afraid to express his or her thoughts and desires of the heart provides an extension of themselves to connect in and grow with one another.

Genuine love has the power to transform people! It was Agape love that went to the cross for us and its agape love filling us when the power of the Holy Spirit indwells us. It causes us to love boldly.

"After they had eaten breakfast, Jesus asked Simon Peter, "Simon, son of John, do you love me more than the other disciples do?" Peter answered him, "Yes, Lord, you know that I love you." Jesus told him, "Feed my lambs." Jesus asked him again, a second time, "Simon, son of John, do you love me?" Peter answered him, "Yes, Lord, you know that I love you." Jesus told him, "Take care of my sheep." Jesus asked him a third time, "Simon, son of John, do you love me?" Peter felt sad because Jesus had asked him a third time, "Do you love me?" So, Peter said to him, "Lord, you know everything. You know that I love you." Jesus told him, "Feed my sheep." John 21:15-17 (GOD'S WORD Translation)

The first two times Jesus asked Peter about his love for Him, the word He used for love was translated, 'agape'. Peter's response to Jesus in how he loved Him was the word used for 'phileo' love. In other words, Jesus was asking Peter, do you love me with a love that can endure anything? A sacrificial love? Peter's reply to Jesus' questions was that he loved him with the affection that one has for a friend. The third time Jesus asked Peter if he loved Him, he asked His question using the type of love that Peter could respond in agreement with, 'do you love me with *phileo* love?'.

Initially, Peter could only answer Jesus with a response verifying phileo love. The proof of the type of love Peter felt for Jesus *at that time* was evident in the three times he denied Christ. The fear in Peter about the consequences he would face for his connection with Jesus, was greater than the type of love he felt for Him. Later, after Peter was filled with the power of the Holy Spirit he received a new boldness and it was *at that time* his love for Jesus shifted from phileo to agape. No one with less than agape love for someone else could willingly go to a death such as Peter endured for his faith in Jesus. That's the transforming power of the Lord filling imperfect people with His perfect Spirit which is; perfect love.

I suspect for the most part, we've been loving one another with a type of phileo love, mistaking it for agape love. Why do I say that?

Very few of us are willing to go to the cross for one another. I believe, very soon that statement will be changing into, 'we've been loving one another with agape love'. As, we are on the verge of a holy revolution of greater boldness in the Spirit – which leads us into loving one another with a greater display of boldness!

"This is My commandment, that you love and unselfishly seek the best for one another, just as I have loved you. No one has greater love [nor stronger commitment] than to lay down his own life for his friends." John 15:12-13 (Amplified Bible)

From (agape) love, we were given life and born again into abundant life. Therefore, to give (agape) love to one another is to nurture with the power to transform what has been dead and dormant into that which flourishes with abundant life. Love never takes, yet it receives; it does not withhold, rather, it gives generously; it is not selfish but selfless; it has the power to heal the deepest wounds and to forgive the most painful offenses; with all that it is, it is also – *always*, a decision.

"We know that we have passed out of death into Life, because we love the brothers and sisters. He who does not love remains in [spiritual] death. Everyone who hates (works against) his brother [in Christ] is [at heart] a murderer [by God's standards]; and you know that no murderer has eternal life abiding in him. By this we know [and have come to understand the depth and essence of His precious] love: that He [willingly] laid down His life for us [because He loved us]. And we ought to lay down our lives for the believers. But whoever has the world's goods (adequate resources), and sees his brother in need, but has no compassion for him, how does the love of God live in him? Little children (believers, dear ones), let us not love [merely in theory] with word or with tongue [giving lip service to compassion], but in action and in truth [in practice and in sincerity, because practical acts of love are more than words]. By this we will know [without any doubt] that we are of the truth, and will assure our heart and quiet our conscience before Him."
1 John 3:14-19 (Amplified Bible)

When we love only with our emotions the filters in our minds every now and then want to tell us certain people don't deserve our unconditional love. Why? If we're being transparent we can admit, we are all flawed people with issues. Some with more issues than others, and some with issues that are merely easier to see than others. Sometimes, when we see those issues in one another, through a religious filter in our mind we begin to cast judgement on the value and worth of that person, thus making a conclusion that they're not worthy of our unconditional love or sacrifice of any kind.

Jesus - not religion or any other kind of flawed mindset – is our example of what love looks like. He displays to us how we are to love one another. Agape love is genuine love. Genuine love is so strong it overcame the grave! The law of the Old Covenant is fulfilled through love. Genuine – agape love is what the new covenant is all about and has the power to transform.

Signs, miracles and wonders will grab the attention and will even bring a person to be a believer in the power of God. Those amazing things will put a testimony in the mouth of a person, but it's genuine love that will transform and can soften even the hardest hearted person. The signs may bring proof that God is in the house but love is what testifies of who we belong to.

What is love? Love is so strong and powerful enough it's eternal. It's revered to the utmost value that every gift of power, every act of generosity, every sign is without worth if not all done upon the foundation of love. Love is the most powerful force there is, and yet it is the most delicate and beautiful gift. It is an incredible treasure worth more than what the mind and heart can perceive without divine revelation. Unconditional (aka; true) love is a constant not a variable. It loves at all times.

On the other hand, put love at the foundation of every manifested gift, sign, miracle, act of charity, and you have released what speaks life into the person's entire being. Friends, genuine agape love is life-giving! Love is the only attribute that's carried over into eternity.

The Spirit and LOVE.... why? God is Spirit and Love and His presence breathes life! What does life-giving love look like?

"Love is very patient and kind, never jealous or envious, never boastful or proud, never haughty or selfish or rude. Love does not demand its own way. It is not irritable or touchy. It does not hold grudges and will hardly even notice when others do it wrong. It is never glad about injustice, but rejoices whenever truth wins out. If you love someone, you will be loyal to him no matter what the cost. You will always believe in him, always expect the best of him, and always stand your ground in defending him." 1Corinthians 13:4-7 *(Living Bible)*

I'm not saying to love like this will be easy. It goes against our natural man much of the time, therefore we must be surrendered to the Spirit-man. It requires self-control, preferring others before ourselves even to the point of swallowing our pride for their sake. It requires us to do the best we can to see from their point of view, to try with all our might to understand their heart instead of their outward behavior. Yes, it will require effort and intentional forgiveness, repeatedly. If you haven't figured it out by now, let me break it to you; you've been enrolled in the hands on, interactive – "Love They Brother 101" course and study. There's a test every day and pop quizzes randomly throughout each day. For every theory study, there's also a practical application of it that follows! Passing this course requires much from us but the reward far outweighs all else. For eternity.

If we desire to see a powerful manifestation of God's kingdom upon the earth – I'm talking signs, miracles and wonders, resurrections, etc. – then let's get back to love. Genuine love as the foundation for every motive, for every function of the gifts we've been given. What if we release our gifts for the sake of love, not because of notoriety or because it's exciting or any reason other than - love. Love is the reason behind the power of the Gospel.

The Spirit of the Lord said to me, *"These are Kingdom fundamentals to those who are mature sons in the Kingdom"*; Luke 6:27-38 *"Listen, all of you. Love your enemies do good to those who hate you. Pray for the happiness of those who curse you; implore God's blessing on those who hurt you. "If someone slaps you on one cheek, let him slap the other too! If someone demands your coat, give him your shirt besides. Give what you have, to anyone who asks you for it; and when things are taken away from you, don't worry about getting them back. Treat others as you want them to treat you. "Do you think you deserve credit for merely loving those who love you? Even the godless do that! And if you do good only to those who do you good—is that so wonderful? Even sinners do that much! And if you lend money only to those who can repay you, what good is that? Even the most wicked will lend to their own kind for full return! "Love your enemies! Do good to them! Lend to them! And don't be concerned about the fact that they won't repay. Then your reward from heaven will be very great, and you will truly be acting as sons of God: for he is kind to the unthankful and to those who are very wicked. "Try to show as much compassion as your Father does. "Never criticize or condemn—or it will all come back on you. Go easy on others; then they will do the same for you. For if you give, you will get! Your gift will return to you in full and overflowing measure, pressed down, shaken together to make room for more, and running over. Whatever measure you use to give—large or small—will be used to measure what is given back to you." (Living Bible)*

God told me, *"The true sons are those who do not despise his brother and those who do not pursue a loftier position because of jealous envy. The sons of the Kingdom are My children who have grown into maturity within their hearts. Maturity involves the giving up of self. Those who possess the ways of My kingdom are those who willingly give up self for the sake of his brother. In those, you will see My kingdom be made manifest. There is no other way My dear children, except to love your brother and in loving, you shall prefer one another over self. Regardless of what the mouth speaks, this is only accomplished by first loving your Lord, your God, above all else.*

75

There are no exceptions, for I, the Lord, peel back every layer to see clearly into the innermost hidden place of the heart. I see with a perfect vision. I beckon unto you, My Church, lay aside every filth and every stench of quarrelsome flesh, that I may take you into the season of mature and ripened fruit in My house. I am calling forth the Bride that is perfected in My ways of love. Do not be discouraged My Bride, even in this you are growing and moving along in the swiftness of My Spirit. I have seen your willingness, and as your understanding increases, you shall shine more brightly and increase in kingdom power. It's (in) the understanding of My love, to love."

Webster defines the word *"fundamental"* in the following way; *Of or pertaining to the foundation or basis; essential; A principle, law or article which serves as the groundwork of a system; essential part.* With this definition in mind, the Lord is telling us His instructions He gave in Luke 6:27-38 is the foundation that must be laid before we can become *mature* sons of the kingdom. This selfless behavior is the solid foundation by which all else of the Kingdom must be built upon. It's totally impossible to be selfless without genuine love.

"Your strong love for each other will prove to the world that you are my disciples." John 13:35 (Living Bible)

Real love produces the desire and the ability to bless others void of any motive of personal gain. The opposite is true when the blessing is given and only the *outward* appearance is of selflessness. If there is a hidden motive in the heart behind the blessing, there will be a desire for recognition in return. How many times have we given a gift and in turn mentioned later, 'and they didn't even thank me for it.'? We did not give the gift without expecting something in return. Perhaps we desired the recognition, even if it was as small as a 'thank you'. Please don't get me wrong, I totally appreciate a 'thank you', and strongly believe a response of gratitude is necessary for affirming and edifying one another. When the response becomes the focus in our giving it is time to do an accountability check of the motive within our heart. Expecting a simple response in return for giving a gift sounds like such a small matter to be focused on but God says He peels back every layer in our hearts to see the innermost hidden place. That tells us He wants to reveal even the tiniest of areas within our hearts that need to be refined. When we bless with the hidden intent to receive recognition and not out of a place of true love, we are as a clanging cymbal. A clanging cymbal isn't for the purpose to make a lovely sound for others to hear, it's for drawing attention.

"If I speak with human eloquence and angelic ecstasy but don't love, I'm nothing but the creaking of a rusty gate. If I speak God's Word with power, revealing all his mysteries and making everything plain as day, and if I have faith that says to a mountain, "Jump," and it jumps, but I don't love, I'm nothing. If I give everything I own to the poor and even go to the stake to be burned as a martyr, but I don't love, I've gotten nowhere. So, no matter what I say, what I believe, and what I do, I'm bankrupt without love."
1 Corinthians 13:1-3 (The Message)

If we - the Church, truly desire the fullness of His inheritance in which we may be considered trustworthy sons and stewards, we must have His love established as the foundation in our hearts. We long to attain and walk in the Kingdom inheritance. We teach and talk about it being ours to lay hold of, and it does belong to us! We must first recognize that it's not for our selfish gain. It's for our victory and for the victory of those in our path. We do not attain it to focus on ourselves.

Our Father delights in blessing us beyond our wildest imaginations, so yes of course there are rewards, blessings and perks in being the King's heirs. When the Spirit of the Lord fills us He brings transformation to us. He never intended for us to keep Him locked up within us, reserved only for ourselves. I have found that when I get excited about something fun or beautiful or even when I've come across something I think works for me in an exceptionally effective way, I can't wait to share it with everyone else so they can experience the same joy. That's exactly what the Lord wants us to do with all He has given to us – share every gift and the joy we have found in Him. Not everyone I share my excitement with gets excited over the same things I do but there are always a few who find the same delight. When I come across those who do it's an awesome time!

Notice the scriptures in Luke 4:18-19; *"The Spirit of the Lord is with me. He has anointed me to tell the Good News to the poor. He has sent me to announce forgiveness to the prisoners of sin and the restoring of sight to the blind, to forgive those who have been shattered by sin, to announce the year of the Lord's favor."* (GOD'S WORD Translation)

These scriptures speak of being equipped by the Holy Spirit to do something for the benefit of someone else. With that in mind, are not the gifts, the abundance, the authority, even the revelation just as equally for the benefit of others and for the glory of God? If it were not so Jesus would not have said, *"As you go, spread this message: 'The kingdom of heaven is near.' Cure the sick, bring the dead back to life, cleanse those with skin diseases, and force demons out of people. Give these things without charging, since you received them without paying."*
Matthew 10:7-8 (GOD'S WORD Translation)

It is the heart of the Father that we come to realize, if we are to die to self-daily then we must desire for Kingdom authority and power to be restored to the church *not* for the sake of, 'what can *I* receive from it?', instead, for the sake of, 'what can I give to *others* from it?'. When we come to understand, and apply that concept, that's when God's Kingdom will surely be seen on earth being made manifest through us.

We like to believe we prefer our brothers and sisters, but do we really understand what it means to prefer one another? The Lord told me if I really prefer someone over myself, then I want them to have something better, not just as nice but *better* than what I want for myself. Wow! That's a hard pill to swallow.

Webster's definition of 'prefer' is; *to put in a higher position, rank, or the like; to advance, exalt; promote. To set above or before something else in estimation, favor, or liking; hold in greater favor; like better. To bring, put, or set forward, or before one; To give a preference or priority to.*

"Be devoted to one another with [authentic] brotherly affection [as members of one family], give preference to one another in honor." Romans 12:10 (Amplified Bible)

"Love from the center of who you are; don't fake it. Run for dear life from evil; hold on for dear life to good. Be good friends who love deeply; practice playing second fiddle." Romans 12:9-10 (The Message)

In theory, it sounds simple enough doesn't it? Let's not forget that our brothers and sisters in which we are to prefer aren't only those dear, beloved friends who are very present in our lives but they are also those people who are strangers to us. They are the lovely, as well as the unlovely. They are the ones who with gratitude will see our sacrifices in preferring them and they are the people who with absolutely no gratitude will take from us and behind our backs speak slanderous words about us.

The Lord gave me this scenario and it was an eye opener for me. We will gladly give up our chair for another person and feel good about having preferred our brother but would we give up our last meal to prefer the life of our brother over our own? Would we give up our winning lottery ticket to prefer another? Would we give up center stage so another could be promoted instead of us? Maybe it would be easy for us if it were someone whom we were close with but what if it was that person who has no gratitude or the person who spoke those slanderous things about us?

"I demand that you love each other as much as I love you. And here is how to measure it—the greatest love is shown when a person lays down his life for his friends; and you are my friends if you obey me." John 15:12-14 (Living Bible)

You may say it's a little extreme to talk about literally giving up your life for another. Yes, it probably is for most of us living in North America. During this present time, we may never have to face the decision to give our life for another. For Christians in many other parts of the world the decision to give their life for a brother is a decision they are faced with quite frequently. Not to mention those who serve in our military or civil service departments. Also, keep in mind, giving up your life for another is not limited to giving up your literal breath of life. It covers giving up your own desires for the sake of another who is in need.

Selfless love is the true nature of the love of Jesus. It may not be the easiest or most ideally comfortable path to walk, but with Christ in us it's not an impossible path. It's the path of love Jesus walked for us.

"When we were utterly helpless, Christ came at just the right time and died for us sinners. Now, most people would not be willing to die for an upright person, though someone might perhaps be willing to die for a person who is especially good. But God showed his great love for us by sending Christ to die for us while we were still sinners." Romans 5:6-8 (New Living Translation)

The Lord is strongly beckoning His people by His Spirit to the place of walking in brotherly love. We're at the point of it being crucial for the Body of Christ to grasp the importance and the understanding of selfless love. The Body is being transformed into the Bride of Christ without spot or blemish, and the Kingdom is about to be made manifest on the earth *through* the Body of Christ. Before this can take place, the Body as each individual member must come into a place of walking in selfless love and be made ready as being 'one' in Christ. I'm not saying if someone else refuses to walk in His love that you will be prevented from walking in the Kingdom inheritance. There are two aspects to be seen in this. Number one, for each of us individually to walk in the Kingdom we must choose to love because that's what everything within the Kingdom is about. It's all empowered through the source of Love. The second aspect to look at is the onslaught of the worldwide harvest to come. I truly believe the initiation of it will come through the place of unity and love among the Believers.

Jesus prayed, *"all may be one, as You Father, are in Me, and I in You; that they also may be one in Us, that the world may believe that You sent Me." (John 17:21)*

We must function as one body – the Body of Christ. Not merely in theory, but in action as well. In theory, we seem to have this perfected. Our words certainly sound as if we have accomplished it outstandingly. But if we were to ask our neighbors, our relatives, our co-workers, our friends and acquaintances, would they confirm our preferring of them?

As the Body, we must be able to see the differences between ourselves without viewing them as wrong because of the diversity in how we function. Each member of the Body is created in its own uniqueness, giving opportunity for it be useful and productive, whereas other members aren't necessarily equipped in the same way. Consider this; Which do you find to be of more importance to you, your foot or your hand? They are both very different in function and appearance from one another, but I think you might agree with me, *both* are of equal importance. The foot cannot fulfill the role of the hand nor the hand of the foot. In the same manner, the members of the Body of Christ may look quite differently and have a vast difference of functions from one another but each person is of equal importance. We all have a unique calling that cannot be entirely fulfilled to the same extent by anyone else. When we begin to view one another through the eyes of love we will see how special and valuable each member of the Body is.

It is my opinion that love is not blind nor ignorant. I love my children with all my heart and yet I can see their mistakes and weaknesses, but it does not alter my love for them in any way, shape or form. The truth is, genuine love is stronger and more powerful than all else and will choose NOT to focus upon another's shortcomings. Genuine love sees quite clearly and is a decisive state of being. It chooses to love. Genuine love, (not infatuation, that we so often confuse for love. Infatuation has no backbone for adversity and will seek its own pleasure first.) can see short-comings, but CHOOSES at will to see beyond into what is good. Love chooses to be longsuffering. Love chooses endurance. Love chooses to search for and believe the best in everyone. Those attributes are what keeps love faithful and alive through every trial, tribulation and hardship that WILL at some time or another be thrown at your relationships with your family, friends and significant other.

Yes, we are about to enter one of the greatest and most exciting times the Body of Christ has ever known. The power of the Holy Spirit will be manifested in signs, miracles and wonders, unlike any other time. We will see the greatest harvest of souls being brought into the Kingdom of God than ever before. The signs and wonders might be what initially catches the attention of the world but our love for one another will be what transforms their opinion of who God is. With joyful expectation, we await these things! This much-awaited day will be ushered in as the sons of the Most High abide with one another in the unity of brotherly love and disperse the selfless love of Christ Jesus. We are well equipped for this. His Spirt is love and dwells in us, He's given us the gift of grace and has written a detailed script of *love in action* by which we can commit to following.

LOVE AND LET LOVE!

"Above all, have fervent and unfailing love for one another, because love covers a multitude of sins [it overlooks unkindness and unselfishly seeks the best for others]."
1 Peter 4:8~Amplified Bible

CHAPTER 7

The Power of Unity

"Hear, O Israel! The Lord our God is one Lord!"
Deuteronomy 6:4 (New Life Version)

"So, there are three witnesses in heaven: The Father, the Word and the Holy Spirit, and these three are One" 1 John 5:7
(Amplified Bible, Classic Edition)

Some years ago, I was pondering the Lord being 'one' and yet the Triune Godhead. I don't mind telling you that it seemed beyond my comprehension as I struggled with how it is possible for the Father, Son, and Holy Spirit to be three and yet "one". The very thought boggled my natural mind as it was against anything logical, to say the least. Spiritual truths can be very difficult for our logical minds to comprehend, therefore I asked Him. The Holy Spirit then began to minister to me while I slept at night. His answer to me was quite simple and yet filled with a wealth of revelation. He said, it is by *"the perfection of unity."* The triune Godhead is in such perfect agreement with one another, they function in all they do and in all they say *AS ONE*! How amazing is that? AWESOMELY AMAZING!

Let's look at what the words "perfection of unity" mean when they are defined according to the dictionary. I'm partial to the definition of 'perfection' found in Merriam-Webster's 'Defined for Kid's' version, which is as such; *a quality or condition that cannot be improved; the act of improving something so that it has no flaws; excellence or skill without flaw.* Noah Webster defines the word, 'unity' as *'the state of being one; oneness.'*

Jesus gives us an excellent insight of the Father, Son and Holy Spirit functioning in perfect unity in John 16: 13-15; *"When the Spirit of Truth comes, he will guide you into the full truth. He won't speak on his own. He will speak what he hears and will tell you about things to come. He will give me glory, because he will tell you what I say. Everything the Father says is also what I say. That is why I said, 'He will take what I say and tell it to you."*
(GOD'S WORD Translation)

You see, the Trinity does not strive or compete against one another for position. They are in perfect unity as one. They are ALL saying the same thing because they have no agenda for themselves. Their agenda is love. They have love for mankind and love for one another. God's plan and will for us is we'd be in the same type of unity with one another.

"Then God said, "Let us make humans in our image, in our likeness. Let them rule the fish in the sea, the birds in the sky, the domestic animals all over the earth, and all the animals that crawl on the earth." So, God created humans in his image. In the image of God, he created them. He created them male and female."
Genesis 1:26-27 (GOD'S WORD Translation)

There are two points of interests I want to address from the above scripture. The first one being, once again God refers to them as being plural and then also as singular, - "God". They were three but due to their perfection of unity they were creating as *one*. Secondly, He made us humans in their likeness. Being created in Their likeness means, we have the same potential within us because it was woven into us from the beginning of our creation. Not that we *become* God, but we can become *like* God in our nature because we have His DNA in us. Make sense?

"Now the Lord God said, "It is not good (beneficial) for the man to be alone; I will make him a helper [one who balances him—a counterpart who is suitable and complementary for him."
Genesis 2:18 (Amplified Bible)

The usage of the word "man" in Genesis 2:18 comes from the Hebrew root word, *'adam'*, and is not in direct reference to male or female, rather, it is a general word used for 'mankind'. So, we could translate it as, "It is not good for a person to be alone." You see, from the beginning God's plan has been for each one of us to have others walking alongside of us. Therefore, the Body of Christ is to be joined together as one body. Our natural, physical body as we are aware has many members within its composition, and yet is still one body. It would be an understatement to say there's solid purpose within each member being joined in unity with the rest of the body. That holds true not only with our physical body, but also with the Body of Christ. Especially now in this time, it's crucial to join in unity with the rest of the Body.

In 1Corinthians 12, we read there are diversities of gifts and functions that have been distributed among the members of the Body for the profit of all. Much like our own natural bodies; what would the hand be without the arm, and what would the arm be without the elbow? And what would the upper body be without the feet to take it places? There are so many differences, and yet coming all together to form one complete body for the profit of all its members. The word states, the early church (Acts 4:31-35) came together in such a way they were of 'one heart and soul'. They dwelt together in such unity, even being unified in their possessions, making It possible for no lack to be among them. That's an amazing display of unity!

> *"See how good and pleasant it is when brothers and sisters live together in harmony!"*
> *Psalm 133:1 (GOD'S WORD Translation)*

To be in harmony means *to be in agreement.* I love the definition of harmony! *(Harmony - the combination of different musical notes played or sung at the same time to produce a pleasing sound; a pleasing combination or arrangement of different things ~ Merriam-Webster)*

Notice it's not the combination of the same thing from different places, it's the combining of *different* sounds or things! That, my friend is like a boat-load of revelation right there in that single definition. I don't know about you, but this makes me totally excited!

Harmony is unity and unity means "as one" or "joined". An obvious example of this would be joining your (different) voices together as in singing to make one sound. The result then creates a harmony of voices (aka; a pleasing sound). Our physical bodies although completely joined together has many different characteristics of each part, with many different functions all combined into one body. There are even parts of our physical body that are more sensitive than other parts and that's exactly how it was created to be. So, if we take that and apply it to being the Body of Christ, being in unity doesn't mean that we are all going to have the exact same opinions, or functions, or feelings, etc. What it does mean is we can all function together in our differences and uniqueness's and still be in unity with one another. We know well that we have all been transformed into one body by the redeeming blood of Jesus Christ and the indwelling Spirit of God.

Being one body in unity doesn't mean we will agree on every small detail. We can have differences of opinions and still be in unity. Differing opinions or simply disagreeing is not the problem among the Body of Believers. Neither of those count as division. The enemy has been working overtime trying to con the Body into believing if we have a difference of opinion, then we are not walking in unity. If he can lead us to believe unity has been broken from the get-go, he can detour us from ever moving as one. That's his plan but the truth we are agreeing on now shines a light on his plans and exposes it as the deception it is. Why would the enemy care if we walk in unity or not? He knows we are at our most powerful when unified.

We must become wise as serpents and gentle as doves in understanding this concept of what division truly is, and what is only a difference of opinion. Disagreement is not a problem unless it leads to a root of contention within your heart. Which means, you can't let it go. When contention continues to stir within you it's no longer just a surface disagreement, it then brings bitterness and grows into division. It has at that point penetrated the heart.

God created us each to be unique. We all have different likes and dislikes, different styles of doing what we do. That's a good thing. It's the way we're intended to be. We look differently, we sound differently, shoot - we even smell differently (I'm not saying that's always a good thing, mind ya)! My favorite food may not be yours', your favorite color may not be mine. We have been given different likes and dislikes, as well as spiritual gifts that are intentionally different from one another. These differences were not given to us that we would come against one another because of them. In fact, it was for the opposite reason. Our differences were given to us for edifying, strengthening, and complimenting one another, while one having a strength where another has a weakness for the completion of all. When we put our combinations together we complete each other.

Let's use the alphabet as an example. Within the alphabet are many different letters. Each letter has its own unique shape and sound. Some of the letters may be somewhat alike while others are quite different from the rest. All the letters combined form what we know as the *alphabet*. The alphabet is not a "letter" but it does take *all* the letters to make the alphabet. With the absence of any single letter, it is no longer the alphabet but merely a *portion* of it. On the other hand, a 'letter' is still a letter without the other members of the alphabet. Whether the letters are alone or combined they remain as a letter regardless. Unlike, when removing one letter from the alphabet changes the status of the alphabet to no longer being complete. The whole, needs everyone to make it *whole*. One single letter still has the same function of sound alone but loses the ability to form a larger word in the absence of the others. Each letter has its own specific job to do. It does not match the sound or the shape of any other letter. If so, then it's function would then become null and void, merely becoming a replica of another letter. This is very much likened to the Body of Christ. It's not only one of us that makes up the formation of the Body, it takes all of us. There are many individual parts with distinct appearances, sounds and functions that make up the entire being of the Body. Sure, some look and sound similar but even they are not exact. Then, there are those who are very different from everyone else, and guess what? That's how the Lord intended it to be. It takes all of us functioning and speaking in our own God-given way for the Body to be intact and thriving as it is intended to be. We each have our own function individually of which we do not lose when alone, but neither can we accomplish the greater calling without the other members walking alongside of us who have distinct functions and purposes from ours.

Remember, the same sound coming forth doesn't produce harmony. Harmony is produced by different sounds combined at the same time. We are people meant to be living together in harmony, that means we need to bring all our differences together at the same time producing something pleasant. When the Lord created Adam and Eve, He created them to be in union of marriage. He said, 'the two will become one flesh'. In other words, He wasn't overlooking the fact of them being two individuals, rather, He was speaking into the unity between them. A perfection of unity that would bind the "two" together as if 'one flesh'. This first creation of mankind coming together into unity as one lays the foundation for us. With all our differences across the board, if man and woman/husband and wife – with the vastness of differences there are between the two genders – can be created in the perfection of unity, how can we, His Church - His Body, not be capable of unifying as well. Differences do not divide us unless we purposely allow them to. It's the differences in the male and female genders that when coming together have the capability to form new life. The same likenesses in genders cannot create new life, it takes the differences to do such a miraculous creation. Likewise, with the Body of Christ, it's in the differences coming together as one having the capability to create the miraculous. In the likenesses, we will only find the partial rather than the completion.

We often hear it said that God is establishing His army. Yes, indeed He is. He is teaching us and training us in many different areas that we may be a mighty, undefeatable army. The one main component that all armies MUST have to be "mighty" is - unity. There must be a moving together 'as one' toward the same common goal for there to be victory in the battle.

"Jesus knew their thoughts and said to them, "Every nation divided into groups that fight each other is going to be destroyed. Every city or family divided into groups that fight each other will not stand." Matthew 12:25 (New Life Version)

We see this very well displayed in the process of organ transplants within the natural body. One of the most determining factors of success or failure with an organ transplant is in whether the body will accept or reject the new organ. If it accepts it as one of its own then the body will receive it and function along with it, growing in strength and thereby resulting in edification of itself.

Ephesians 4:16 "He makes the whole body fit together and unites it through the support of every joint. As each and every part does its job, he makes the body grow so that it builds itself up in love." (GOD'S WORD Translation) If the body views the new organ as a foreign object thus rejecting it, it then begins to fight against itself. Sometimes tearing itself down to the point of being the cause of its own death.

Have you ever heard someone say - or maybe even said it yourself - "I have God, I don't need anyone else."? That's a much-too-common deception the enemy loves us to fall prey to. It's much easier for him to take out someone who walks alone, than it is those who walk in numbers. As much as I love to spend quite a bit of alone time with the Lord, I still need people in my life to come alongside me. The truth is we need each other. In my natural body, I would not purposely cut off my own leg. I want both of my legs and I need both to walk and run with ease. My body would no longer be complete with one of my legs gone because one of its members would be missing. Could I still function with only one leg? Of course, but not quite with the same smoothness of mobility that I was originally designed to. If each member of our natural body, which is only temporal, is so highly valuable we wouldn't want to lose one single member, how is it we could disregard any member of the Body of Christ as not having as much value as ourselves (or as the other members) – when we ALL have eternal value.

"As holy people whom God has chosen and loved, be sympathetic, kind, humble, gentle, and patient. Put up with each other, and forgive each other if anyone has a complaint. Forgive as the Lord forgave you. Above all, be loving. This ties everything together perfectly. Also, let Christ's peace control you. God has called you into this peace by bringing you into one body. Be thankful. Let Christ's word with all its wisdom and richness live in you. Use psalms, hymns, and spiritual songs to teach and instruct yourselves about God's kindness. Sing to God in your hearts. Everything you say or do should be done in the name of the Lord Jesus, giving thanks to God the Father through him."
Colossians 3:12-17 (GOD'S WORD Translation)

If we being the Body, who are witnesses of Jesus Christ are bickering and backbiting among ourselves, blocking the view of our love for one another, who of the world will want to listen to us when we testify of Jesus and His love? No one.

"So then, as Christians, do you have any encouragement? Do you have any comfort from love? Do you have any spiritual relationships? Do you have any sympathy and compassion? Then fill me with joy by having the same attitude and the same love, living in harmony, and keeping one purpose in mind. Don't act out of selfish ambition or be conceited. Instead, humbly think of others as being better than yourselves. Don't be concerned only about your own interests, but also be concerned about the interests of others."
Philippians 2:1-4 (GOD'S WORD Translation)

Some years ago, the Lord gave me a vision of how in our diversities we still remain in unity. The picture I saw in this vision was of a cloud of the Holy Spirit filled with the Word of God hovering over many people. Each one of these people stood beside the other one beneath this cloud. The cloud had extensions of itself that reached down into the top of the head of each person beneath it. Although everyone was not connected to one another horizontally, they were each connected vertically to the same cloud of the Holy Spirit/Word thus causing all to be united through the connection of the Holy Spirit. This vision shows us clearly how to stay unified and like-minded as one Body the way we need to be and have been created to be. If we keep our head in the cloud of the Holy Spirit and out of the carnal mindedness of the flesh, then we walk in unity. The flesh and all its carnal mindedness can lead nowhere else except to *self*. 'Self' is the opposite of unity and therefore is the first temptation leading to division. The flesh wants its own way, period. When we allow our flesh to rule over the Spirit we fight to get our own way. Sometimes we fight ourselves. Sometimes we fight God and sometimes we fight each other. But if we walk in the Spirit we put aside those desires of the flesh, which are selfish, and we close all those gaps that allow the enemy to gain access causing division and discord.

We have a real enemy of our soul and it's very important to understand, people are not our enemy. The accuser of our people is the enemy we battle. He disguises himself rather cleverly at times setting the stage to appear as if the other person were the cause of our misfortune. The accuser is always the culprit. He may gain access to influence someone but they are the victim of his deception, therefore our battle is with the accuser not our brothers and sisters in Christ. The Lord spoke into my heart some years ago, *"when His Body comes into genuine love and unity with one another, that's when the revival to bring in the great harvest will take place."* That's why it is so crucial that we get this message not only into our minds but deep within our hearts. The enemy already knows that when we unite he doesn't stand a chance. So, he fights with all the tricks he must, trying to keep us angry and hurt with one another thinking we don't need anyone else. That's nonsense. We do. We were created to be linked with others. When we link together via the Holy Spirit and each person is in unity with Him, we enter a state of being one; a totality of related parts combined, made one by joint action which is, the will of God.

Out of all the topics I've taught and wrote about throughout the years, 'unity' is the one I have the greatest resistance with. Almost every time I get on the computer to type anything out in regard to it I battle with the computer shutting down in error. When I've taught publicly about it, I've been up against false accusations and people suddenly stirring strife. As I gathered notes for this writing I had to print my notes off on three separate occasions, due to their strange disappearance from my desktop. To be in unity with one another is POWERFUL against the forces of darkness that come against our families, our cities, our nations, our churches, our blessings, our Body, and our testimony of Christ to the world. We don't have to agree on all our opinions, but we do have to know we can disagree without being divided from one another.

"Until we're all moving rhythmically and easily with each other, efficient and graceful in response to God's Son, fully mature adults, fully developed within and without, fully alive like Christ. No prolonged infancies among us, please. We'll not tolerate babes in the woods, small children who are an easy mark for impostors. God wants us to grow up, to know the whole truth and tell it in love—like Christ in everything. We take our lead from Christ, who is the source of everything we do. He keeps us in step with each other. His very breath and blood flow through us, nourishing us so that we will grow up healthy in God, robust in love." Ephesians 4:13-16
(The Message)

Everyone is talking about revival. What is it going to look like? How will it be ushered in? How do we know it has begun? I personally believe the answer has been before us all along. It's so obvious and simple but we're missing it as we're searching all over for some complicated and hidden formula. It's not complicated. It's not hidden.

I believe it's what God is all about. When there is genuine, unconditional love there is also grace and when love and grace are active they create unity. When there is true unity among the body, the greatest revival will burst forth like a blazing fire!

The following scriptures are confirming unity and the power it brings to those who choose to walk together as one. With as many people who are included within the context of these scriptures, although they were in unity with one another, I highly doubt every person agreed on every single matter within their daily lives. If I could instill any one thing within your remembrance today, it would be disagreements do not need to create disunity. The lack of grace creates disunity. LOVE + GRACE = UNITY.

"All these with one mind and one purpose were continually devoting themselves to prayer, [waiting together] along with the women, and Mary the mother of Jesus, and with His brothers."
Acts 1:14

"When the day of Pentecost had come, they were all together in one place" Acts 2:1(Amplified Bible)

God has placed some awesome people in my life over the years. He's brought people that have helped me through tough times and celebrated with me in victorious times. They weren't in my life by accident they were purposely placed there as God's provision to me.

When a former ministry partner and I were being established to walk with one another - while each being in our own separate homes the Lord gave us visions. Unknowing that the other one had been given a vision as well, we began to excitedly tell one another about the vision we'd been given. As we were talking almost simultaneously we discovered He had given us both the very same vision!

In the vision, we were both climbing up a mountain together side by side. At times one of the two would become wearied and not able to keep climbing without the other one's help. Whoever had the most strength at the time would reach down and take the other one by the hand and help to lift her up. As we hiked up this mountain we continuously took turns helping one another climb the mountain. Over the years while we partnered together we witnessed that vision play out in our lives. The Lord taught us how to lift one another up that mountain by always pointing each other back to His word.

Most of us have probably heard stories about families who have several boys, be it brothers or cousins who have a reputation for sticking up for one another to no end. They so solidly unite together if you mess with one of them, to your despair you've taken on all of them. The Lord told me that's how it should be with the Body of Christ in regard to the enemy's attacks. We should be so tightly knitted together when the enemy sends an attack against one, he has all of us to contend with. As well as, if we remain tightly knitted together when the accuser of the Body arises to stir strife among us, there will be no place of entry he can access to do his damage.

"Two can accomplish more than twice as much as one, for the results can be much better. If one falls, the other pulls him up; but if a man falls when he is alone, he's in trouble. Also, on a cold night, two under the same blanket gain warmth from each other, but how can one be warm alone?" Ecclesiastes 4:9-11 (Living Bible)

"By yourself you're unprotected.
With a friend you can face the worst.
Can you round up a third?
A three-stranded rope isn't easily snapped."

Ecclesiastes 4:12~The Message

CHAPTER 8

The Weapon of His Word

Pep talks are great, they may be motivational but have no power to transform. Unlike the word of God which is *"living and active"*. There's POWER in the Word! His truth lifts us over and above the circumstances and gives us the strength and hope to continue our ascension up the mountain.

Many years ago, the Lord spoke to me, *"Do not give counsel based on your own opinion. Over the course of time and with more knowledge and maturity, opinion changes. My word is steadfast and does not change. Speak according to My Word."* Truth is always found in God's word and God's word has the power to transform not only our fashion of thinking but also our circumstances and the very atmosphere we live in.

"For the Word that God speaks is alive and full of power; it is sharper than any two-edged sword, penetrating to the dividing line even of soul and spirit; and joints and marrow, exposing and sifting and analyzing and judging the very thoughts and purposes of the heart."
Hebrews 4:12

What does that mean? It means the word of God is an accurately precise weapon in cutting off anything and everything that is deceivingly portraying itself as truth but is an imposter of truth. Deception is tricky and dangerous in that it intertwines itself so closely knitted together with facets of truth that at times it can become difficult to separate the truth from the lie. God's word is so powerfully accurate it can sever between what otherwise is humanly impossible to rightly divide between. What is even more miraculous is while it cuts off the corrupt, it does so without causing damage to that which is good, leaving intact all that is pure and life sustaining. Amazing! No other argument other than the very truth/word of God has the capability of doing that within our lives.

There's an incredible promise to us found in Isaiah 55:10-*11*, *"Rain and snow come down from the sky. They do not go back again until they water the earth. They make it sprout and grow so that it produces seed for farmers and food for people to eat. My word, which comes from my mouth, is like the rain and snow. It will not come back to me without results. It will accomplish whatever I want and achieve whatever I send it to do."*

God is not a man so that He should or for that matter *'could'* lie, so if He says He sent His word that you may be healed then expect to be healed. If He sent His word that you may have life more abundantly then expect it to be just as He has said. There's power in His word to accomplish exactly what He intends for it to do.

His word is so powerful and full of life that even when there was nothing - NOTHING - God spoke and all of creation was formed into existence! And just when you thought it couldn't get any better than that, it does!! The very Spirit of God that spoke everything into existence is living inside of us and He has equipped us with everything we need to overcome any circumstance and roadblock opposing His will for us. I don't know about you, but the very thought of that sends excitement and electric jolts of faith shooting through my core!

"Last of all I want to remind you that your strength must come from the Lord's mighty power within you. Put on all of God's armor so that you will be able to stand safe against all strategies and tricks of Satan. For we are not fighting against people made of flesh and blood, but against persons without bodies—the evil rulers of the unseen world, those mighty satanic beings and great evil princes of darkness who rule this world; and against huge numbers of wicked spirits in the spirit world. So, use every piece of God's armor to resist the enemy whenever he attacks, and when it is all over, you will still be standing up. But to do this, you will need the strong belt of truth

and the breastplate of God's approval. Wear shoes that are able to speed you on as you preach the Good News of peace with God. In every battle, you will need faith as your shield to stop the fiery arrows aimed at you by Satan. And you will need the helmet of salvation and the sword of the Spirit—which is the Word of God."

Ephesians 6:10-17 (Living Bible)

I want you to take notice of something in this - all the armor being placed on you; the helmet, belt, shield, breastplate, shoes - when all properly secured on us is to *protect* us from what the enemy fires at us. It's very important that it's all in its place so we won't be harmed. But this one weapon - the *sword of the Spirit*, being the word of God is the weapon that makes us dangerous to the enemy and his plans. The enemy doesn't tremble when he sees our armor in place. The armor is protection and is vital for us to have it secured but it's when the enemy sees us wielding the sword - the word of God, *that's* when he trembles! When in battle it's not the armor that causes injury and death to the enemy, it's the sword. So then, how do we wield the sword? Jesus tells us in Mark 11:23; *"For assuredly, I say to you, whoever says to this mountain, 'Be removed and be cast into the sea,' and does not doubt in his heart, but believes that those things he says will be done, he will have whatever he says".*

God's word is the weapon and faith is the substance that activates it unto power. It is the weapon in which we overcome all that rises against us and faith activates the weapon. We must speak aloud declaring the word into our circumstances, simply believing God at His word. There's power in His logos word, (the written word - the scriptures), and His rhema word, (the word spoken to us by the Holy Spirit, as in a prophetic promise). His rhema word will always agree with His logos word. If you recall, the Word and the Holy Spirit are both only speaking what they hear the Father speak.

The word of the Lord is effective and sure but sometimes there are delays as to what we perceive should be a sufficient amount of time for the word to manifest. When the delay goes past the span of time which seems logical to us, we begin to wonder if the word is as point-on as the Lord said. There may also be the case when we've received a prophetic word from someone else and it has taken so long to come to fruition we begin to think they missed it and spoke from their own imagination.

I understand the discouragement of prolonged waiting on a promise from the Lord, but keep in mind our timing is not the same as God's. His word is timeless and does not expire merely because we think it should have gone out of date. I have words from legitimate prophets that seemed so far-fetched to me at the time they were given, I couldn't find a witness within myself as being genuinely for me. It wasn't that I thought they weren't speaking from the Holy Spirit, I just could not associate their words anywhere in my life. Some of what was prophesied to me about situations and people in my life was totally opposite of what the natural reality for me was at that time. Then my life looked completely different than what it does now. Fifteen years later, I am experiencing those prophetic words manifesting in my life and can clearly understand how perfectly they fit with where my life currently. If I had written those words off as false or as missing the mark because nothing seemed to be real in them for me then I may have wrongly discredited the prophetic people who delivered what turned out to be very accurate words – many years later. I also would have been dishonoring the Holy Spirit, who speaks to us what He hears the Father saying. Whatever delays seem to be within the time between the word spoken and the fruition of it, it is of utmost importance we stand firmly on God's word above the appearance which may be speaking something opposite to us.

"A man's stomach will be satisfied with the fruit of his mouth; He will be satisfied with the consequence of his words. Death and life are in the power of the tongue, And those who love it and indulge it will eat its fruit and bear the consequences of their words." Proverbs 18:20-21 (Amplified Bible)

Not only has the Lord given us power in speaking His word, also in our place of unity He's given us the power of agreement.

"I can guarantee again that if two of you agree on anything here on earth, my Father in heaven will accept it." Matthew 18:19
(GOD'S WORD Translation)

Gen. 11:1-6 "*Now the whole earth used the same language and the same words. And as men traveled in the east, they found a valley in the land of Shinar and made their home there. They said to one another, "Come, let us make blocks and burn them until they are hard." They used blocks for stone, and tar to hold them together. Then they said, "Come, let us build a city for ourselves, with a tower that touches the heavens. Let us make a name for ourselves, or else we may be sent everywhere over the whole earth." Then the Lord came down to see the city and the tower that the sons of men had built. And the Lord said, "See, they are one people, and they all have the same language. This is only the beginning of what they will do. Now all they plan to do will be possible for them."*
(New Life Version)

Although, the building of the tower of Babel was an unrighteous agreement, because the people were *as one* God said, 'nothing they proposed to do would be withheld from them'. Being an unrighteous agreement as it was it was void of God's blessing and power, therefore He sent His hand against it and brought it to an end along with dividing the people across the land.

Let's suppose we - being the Body of Christ, purposed to come together in righteous agreement declaring God's word. Agreeing with what God says would have His blessing and power working with us. Even so much as going before us. In that case, what might we be able to accomplish together - as one, declaring His powerful word into our circumstances? When we begin to come together in such a way, *that's* when we will see our households, our schools, our workplaces, communities, government, and even nations transformed. I can personally testify of this power of agreement with others in the Body of Christ and the word of God. In my own life, it has powerfully brought many breakthroughs, at times literally overnight.

100

"I pray that all of these people continue to have unity in the way that you, Father, are in me and I am in you. I pray that they may be united with us so that the world will believe that you have sent me. I have given them the glory that you gave me. I did this so that they are united in the same way we are. I am in them, and you are in me. So, they are completely united. In this way, the world knows that you have sent me and that you have loved them in the same way you have loved me." John 17:21 23 God's Word Translation

CHAPTER 9

Be Your Brother's Keeper

The Holy Spirit says, *"Happy is the man who in his heart makes melody to the Lord."*

"Don't drink too much wine, for many evils lie along that path; be filled instead with the Holy Spirit and controlled by him. Talk with each other much about the Lord, quoting psalms and hymns and singing sacred songs, making music in your hearts to the Lord. Always give thanks for everything to our God and Father in the name of our Lord Jesus Christ. Honor Christ by submitting to each other." Ephesians 5:18-21 (Living Bible)

The Lord told me, *"In this manner, worship and give honor to the King of Glory"*, *(in the manner of Ephesians 5:18-21).* We may not normally consider our interaction with others as a form of worship and honor to Jesus, but why not? In the above scripture, notice the direction given is an intermingling of edifying one another and exalting the Lord. That's because Jesus is the Head and born again-Believers are His Body. The Body is connected to the Head and with that being so, how can we define the two as being separate from one another? I believe God wants us to view the Body of Christ as just what it is - *the* Body of Christ. Of course, He is not telling us to worship people, we are to worship God and Him alone, but I do believe He is telling us to stop looking at all the flaws in one another and instead look at the 'Jesus" in our Born-Again brothers and sisters. When we can learn to see the Jesus in one another we can then truly serve one another in the Lord, edifying one another in the love and respect and honor as is due any member of the Body of Jesus. Jesus said the two greatest commandments are; first and foremost - to love God with all our heart and all that we are, and secondly - to love one another just as we love ourselves. The Lord doesn't give the commandment to only love Him but He is also giving the commandment to love His Body. You see, we are not just merely His creation. Trees, mountains, rivers are all His creations. We are members of His body which make us a part of Him. An extension of Him, if you will!

The Holy Spirit told me, *"As you allow the King of Glory to abide and sweep clean your heart, you will be transformed from glory to glory. (In) putting aside the dullness of the worldly knowledge (earthly wisdom), you will be renewed in the mind of Christ that the glory of He who is above all else will fill and surround you. Is it possible? Oh yes! More than possible, readily available and waiting on you. The presence of the King is coming to My people in an unveiled way that has not before been known or recognized."*

"But whenever anyone turns to the Lord from his sins, then the veil is taken away. The Lord is the Spirit who gives them life, and where he is there is freedom from trying to be saved by keeping the laws of God. But we Christians have no veil over our faces; we can be mirrors that brightly reflect the glory of the Lord. And as the Spirit of the Lord works within us, we become more and more like him."
    2 Corinthians 3:16-18 (Living Bible)

The Lord has been doing a magnificent work in the Church within this last decade especially. The greatest transformation is nearing its time to be seen. He has been steadily removing the dullness of hearing and the cloudiness of vision, by bringing us out of a position of 'doing' church and into 'being' the church. There is an evident change taking place in the hearts of born again Believers who have been realizing that 'doing' church keeps us in a position of legalistic programs. We are discovering, 'being' His church liberates us into a position of walking in an intimate relationship with the King of Glory. This is not just another 'new Christian movement' taking place that will quickly pass away. This is a true Holy Spirit transformation taking place in the heart of each individual member of the Body. And yet, because it's individuals that make up the corporate body, the corporate church is about to enter the most powerful transformation that has been seen up to this time moving from glory to glory. Some may call it REVIVAL! Other's may call it RESTORATION! Or, you might call it REVOLUTION OF THE HOLY SPIRIT! It's all of those, so whichever it is to you, call it what you may.

He said to me, *"This is the time of the latter rain. Let the people declare; 'Open up! Open up you, heavens and pour out the rain! Pour out the rain upon the earth!'"* There is an abundance coming by the Spirit of the Lord. The people of God are about to be refreshed by His Spirit being made able to enter His peace and His rest through knowing Him - really knowing Him. The lord has shown me the wind of the Holy Spirit moving across the face of the earth, leaving nothing untouched. Not one will be left out from the 'opportunity' of being touched by the very Spirit of God. Not all will receive for many will choose to reject the truth therefore rejecting the wind of the Spirit, but *all* will be given the opportunity.

God said to me, *"There's a fresh and exciting unity and sense of agreement by My Spirit coming upon My Body that will break the entanglement and yoke of dissension. In this right unity, you will see a greater depth of anointing flowing to bring deliverance and liberty. The presence of the King of Glory is coming and restoring all things to Him. Look up once again Church, for your redemption draws near."* As the Lord spoke this to me He showed me the holy priesthood. I believe He showed it to me because the Bride is being purified. There is a purging of the ways and influences of society that the Bride has at times willingly accepted and therefore it has caused Her to show traces of what is not of our Savior. We are being cleansed and there is a generation that is now emerging and taking their positions of intolerance to compromise. They are a people who is committed to stay pure and their focus is undivided. The Word is written on the tablets of their hearts. This is not a promise of a generation limited to a certain age group, gender, religious denomination, nationality, or of a certain status and position. This generation consists of both young and old, male and female, all nations of people, great and small, ALL who are willing to seek the face of the Lord.

"The earth is the Lord's, and all that is in it, the world, and all who live in it. For He has built it upon the seas. He has set it upon the rivers. Who may go up the mountain of the Lord? And who may stand in His holy place? He who has clean hands and a pure heart. He who has not lifted up his soul to what is not true, and has not made false promises. He will receive what is good from the Lord, and what is right and good from the God Who saves him. Such is the family of those who look for Him, who look for Your face, O God of Jacob. Lift up your heads, O gates. And be lifted up, O doors that last forever. And the King of shining-greatness will come in. Who is the King of shining-greatness? The Lord strong and powerful. The Lord powerful in war. Lift up your heads, O gates. Lift them up, O doors that last forever and the King of shining-greatness will come in. Who is the King of shining-greatness? The Lord of All. He is the King of shining-greatness." Psalm 24 (New Life Version)

There have been several occasions the Lord has spoken to me through the numbers on the clock, just as He does with many other people as well. If you have never received revelation from Him in this manner of communication, then it might seem slightly odd and possibly wavering on the side of *imagination*. I understand those questioning thoughts because in the past I also have had them a time or two. I've had my moments of doubting if those types of occurrences are really from God or perhaps an overactive imagination. If you find, the way I have received this revelation seems too ridiculous for you to receive from it, then may I suggest you look past the method and merely focus on the message? There are times the Lord has instructed me to do that when the method was more like a stumbling block to my doubting mind, which was in effect keeping my mind and my heart from receiving a valid message from the Lord. Not all receive the voice of the Holy Spirit in the same manner, and in our humanity sometimes when we encounter something new it feels strange enough to seem false. Keep in mind, the first impression does not validate it as being false. It's merely different from our own personal experiences and understanding.

Usually, when the Lord is speaking a message to me from the numbers on the clock it comes in the form of repetition. My progression in understanding, can at times be slow in realizing I'm supposed to be getting revelation from the time on the clock. Yep, that 'aha!" moment doesn't always come all too quickly for me, I'm sorry to say. Normally, I'll repeatedly be drawn to look at the clock when it's the same time so frequently, I eventually come to understand there's something more to this than merely coincidence. Except for this time, it hit me like a ton of bricks! Very quickly I understood the Lord wanted me to see something within the numbers He had drawn my attention to. At that time in my life, I was a mail carrier for a rural mail route and was working that morning. I felt led to glance at the clock/stereo in the dashboard of the car I was driving. As prodded in my spirit, I took a glance and just as quickly looked away without much thought of it. As I turned my eyes elsewhere it felt like everything within me woke up to what I had seen in that moment. It sunk in, the Lord was speaking to me and jolted me with what felt like a sense of adrenaline pouring through my entire being. I took another look to verify what I thought I saw was indeed correct. The numbers being displayed on the radio (94.5) and on the digital clock (9:45) were the same. I knew the Holy Spirit had called my attention to it but still did not understand why and what it was about. The following morning on the way to church I felt a nudging to once again look at the time. I glanced over at the clock display on the dashboard of our vehicle and noticed the time read, "9:42". Then, I heard the Lord speak into my spirit, *"look at the time on your phone instead"*. The time on my phone read "9:45", which was the same numerical formation He wanted me to see the day prior.

God is merciful and kind and wants nothing but the best for us. He has called us to be victorious and His plan for us is for a good future and success in everything He leads us into. He has given us open access to a beautiful and personal relationship with Him. He has given us His kingdom and all the treasure within. He has given us His

Spirit, His name, His Word, and everything good. Unfortunately, those things are not always manifesting in our daily lives. They should be and He wants them to be, obviously – that's the reason He gave them to us. He wants them to be manifesting as a normal part of our life, even more than we do. Being the merciful, patient Father He is, He's giving us a heads-up you might say. He wants us to be clear of the time and season we are entering.

In my spirit, I hear Him speaking, 'it is a time of self-accountability'. Notice, I said, "self", which means, we're not to be peering into our neighbor's life to point out what needs to be changed with them. "Self" accountability means we are to judge ourselves through the word of God and the gentle, yet effectiveness of the Holy Spirit within us. When the Father gives a rebuke it's not for us to point a finger at the other person and say, 'oh that's for them!'. Clearly, He wants us to look within ourselves. Not them.

It's a possibility we may not be seeing the kingdom of heaven manifesting in our daily lives because we're holding onto things in our lives that are not of His kingdom. It may be; not forgiving someone else or ourselves, wrong mindsets or willful sin. Whatever the reason is, it's time to take an internal account and allow the Holy Spirit to show each one of us what it is we need to remove from our lives.

"If your hand or your foot gets in God's way, chop it off and throw it away. You're better off maimed or lame and alive than the proud owner of two hands and two feet, godless in a furnace of eternal fire. And if your eye distracts you from God, pull it out and throw it away. You're better off one-eyed and alive than exercising your twenty-twenty vision from inside the fire of hell." Mark 9:45-48 (The Message)

"They crush Your people, O Lord, and afflict and abuse Your heritage." Psalm 94:5 (Amplified Bible)

There is nothing in this world worth keeping us from walking in the fullness of relationship and the presence of the Lord. Walking in the fullness with Him also means walking in the fullness of His kingdom. His presence ushers in His kingdom and His presence IS where His kingdom exists.

What is it that holds us back from Him? Sin! What is sin? Anything that separates us from a full relationship with Him and His best for us. As well as, whatever steers us away from the Lord and His truth, and that may very well be different things to different people. What separates me from a full relationship with Him most likely is slightly different than what separates you. How so? For example, if a person has an addiction to caffeine they are then being controlled by their intake of specific products containing caffeine, which is causing damage to their health, for one. That person may be disobeying the voice of the Lord every time they choose to drink a soda. Whereas, someone else may not have the same weakness and drinking an occasional caffeinated drink isn't causing them to stumble. That may seem like a generic example, but I believe it presents the point at hand. We all have different issues to deal with in our lives. What may be as sin to one isn't necessarily a sin to another.

Please don't misunderstand, there are obvious actions that are sin to all and that's not what I am referring to. Of course, cold-blooded murder is sin because it defies the commandment of love. So, I am in no way saying murder is wrong to one but not to another. Although, murder and killing are not one in the same, there is a matter of the heart that separates the two but that's for another time. (Self-defense is not murder, for example)

Each one of us should take an internal accountability for our own thoughts, actions and motives of the heart. Those things we hold onto that are stumbling blocks and sin in disguise are the very things that crush us (as stated in Psalm 94) and are an affliction upon us. We may not recognize them as such but they are holding us back from the heritage of the Lord.

The definition of *heritage* is: *something that comes or belongs to one by reason of birth; an inherited lot or portion. (Word Reference definition)*

God wants us to have all that He has. What is His is ours by right of being born-again into His Kingdom. The stumbling blocks we have placed in our own way (some knowingly and some unknowingly – because of lack of knowledge) are holding us back from His best for us. In His loving mercy, He is giving us this appointed season, to more easily and readily have eyes to see what those sins are within our own lives. If we choose to depart from them and cut them off, in this season there is also a heightened atmosphere of grace being released upon us, likened to the blood of the lamb upon the doorposts during Passover.

Ask for eyes to see and wisdom to discern whatever may be in your own life holding you back from the fullness. With an open heart, recognize and acknowledge to the Lord what He's shown you and set your heart and mind on cutting them off from any further connection and influence in your life. Just as the angel of death passed over those who had the blood of the lamb upon their doorpost, the Spirit of the Lord will triumph over your stumbling block and deliverance will come much faster and with less struggle than what it has in past experiences. Tis the season of grace for deliverance. Go for it! You have nothing to lose, (except extra baggage weighing you down) and an entire kingdom to gain. God's light doesn't only shine into the dark areas of the world around us it also shines into the dark areas of the world within us.

"So, what a blessing when God steps in and corrects you! Mind you, don't despise the discipline of Almighty God!" Job 5:17
(The Message)

Hebrews 12: 7; "Let God train you, for he is doing what any loving father does for his children. Whoever heard of a son who was never corrected?" (v 11) "Being punished isn't enjoyable while it is happening—it hurts! But afterwards we can see the result, a quiet growth in grace and character." (Living Bible)

Several years ago, when I was co-pastoring a small church, the Lord told me to take this rebuke to the congregation, *"The Body of Christ has been praying soulish prayers and it's time for it to stop."* I can't say It was a teaching I was most excited about delivering. At that time, I wasn't very well informed on what soulish prayers looked like, so it was a new avenue the Lord was taking me down to lead others in. No pressure, of course…. Whatever! Only about as much as a pressure cooker! (wink)

Accountability among other members of the Body we each have been given to walk closely with is a good thing. There is a righteous accountability to be walked in alongside one another, but let me be clear in saying; accountability is not control, nor is it as much about a person making mistakes and being human as it is about how well we love one another.

To be your *brother's keeper* does not give you dictatorship over him. It means, you look out for his best interests and protect him. That would include protecting him from the backbiters, the slanderers (even if he's doing something off-kilter), and yes, it would be lovingly talking to him about something you feel may be dragging him down from receiving God's best. If that last reason is not initiated from a heart of total love, then it's not driven by the Holy Spirit and should not be done. Not agreeing with someone's decisions in their own life (decisions that are not sinful and damaging) is not our business to try to hold them accountable for what we feel they should be doing differently. That's control and is quite different.

I have heard many times over the years, not necessarily limited to leaders of the church, but people in general addressing what they perceive as being 'issues' with someone else and bringing it forth saying they are holding them in accountability. They do this under the belief they are only doing what they're supposed to, by exposing whatever it is to the targeted person and possibly to others also. The real issue in this, is what may have begun as sincere concerns evolved into nitpicking. When dealing with the so-called *holding one another accountable for sins* we tend to roam into holding one another accountable for the pet-peeves that annoy us about the other person and frankly, it has nothing to do with sin whatsoever. Nor is it protecting our brother and sister as their keeper.

Conviction is an accountability to the Spirit of God. There can be several ways God will bring conviction to His people; the written word or another person speaking by the leading of the Holy Spirit, which in most cases that'd be someone who already has an established relationship with them, but not always. The most common way I have witnessed conviction from the Lord is by the Holy Spirit speaking directly to the person, Himself. How ever it may be that God brings conviction to His people, there is one ingredient that is always the same – it brings liberty to the person receiving it. *Receiving* is the key word. For the liberty to happen the person must receive it as truth in their heart.

On the other hand, condemnation is heavy and oppressing because it is a passing of judgment; GUILTY AS CHARGED WITH NO HOPE OF BEING PARDONED. Just like conviction, condemnation can be brought to you by another person or brought on by yourself. The difference is, conviction is a righteous judgment that brings liberty and hope when received. Condemnation is like a heavy weight of mud being laid on top of you. It feels like no matter what you do or however many times you repent, you cannot get clean.

I am most certain over the years, especially through my 'religious' years, I was a partaker in bringing the heavy hand of condemnation upon people. It was done in ignorance and from the lofty mindset religion tends to steer us toward. I cannot undo whatever I may have said or muttered to God about them in the past, but now - with a heart of love and not religion, issuing grace to myself and others is much more readily accessible. I've been under the scrutiny of condemnation many times, and often still am. I can tell you It's not pleasant. It does not bring about anything positive, it only damages.

One of the symptoms of carrying a judgment of condemnation is not only do you view most everyone else through the lens of condemnation, you are also your own worst condemner. If you can't issue grace to others, you certainly cannot issue it to yourself either. If I had to choose which end is the greater of the two evils; the receiving or the giver, I would have to say, 'the giver'. Being on the end of the stick where condemnation is being flung at you is painful but being the condemner is sin and comes with repercussions (Judge not.)

When the Lord told me to address the 'nit-picking', He explained to me why we refer to it as nit-picking. A nit is extremely tiny and very difficult to see. You must literally pick through someone's hair with a fine-tooth comb, combing almost each strand of hair individually. It's a search that's done with intentions of finding every little nettling thing. In other words, when you nit-pick you are intentionally searching for the speck in your brother's eye.

It's my opinion that most soulish prayers do not begin from a heart of malice, more than likely they originate from good intentions. Although God is merciful in our ignorance, He doesn't want us to remain in our state of ignorance not discerning a soulish prayer from a Spirit-led one. His desire is for us to know truth and to be free to grow and mature as the 'sons' He's called us to be.

Soulish prayers are prayers prayed apart from being led by the Holy Spirit. They may be prayers that involve *our* will rather than *God's* will. They might be prayers of a personal content or those prayed for other individuals, churches or ministries. Sometimes, they might begin with God's will then venture into a prayer that is taking on the form of controlling the other person into something we want for them, as opposed to what they want or what God wants. Most likely, the person praying such a prayer isn't aware they are doing so. Their intentions aren't for harm, in fact probably the very opposite. They see a situation and feel they have the correct answer for the best of everyone. Sound familiar? To be frank, soulish prayers can be a form of witchcraft. It may sound a bit harsh or absurd to think that God's people might be praying witchcraft prayers. Unfortunately, it's not as absurd as you think. I don't mean witchcraft in the sense of someone chanting evil incantations over an innocent victim. Let me explain, God has given us our own free will. He designed a plan for each of our lives that entails His perfect will. He will never impose His will on us in such a way it overrides the free will He gave to us. He does not force us to submit to Him. He may allow circumstances to be contributing factors for our decisions, but He never forces us into submission. He does not manipulate either. He will beckon and urge and ask, but not control us. Witchcraft is a form of control over another person's will so anytime someone else is superimposing their will upon another person it's a form of witchcraft or a controlling spirit, rather than the Spirit of God.

When the Lord begins to move upon people bringing the liberty of His Spirit it does not necessarily 'look' like what we expected it to look like. Much of the time we don't recognize it's from Him when it comes. The old ways of doing things even in the areas we were in bondage to, are what we can be most comfortable with as they are the most familiar to us. How many times have we believed the way we did what we did was the 'right' way, and those people over there were doing it the wrong way? God can be moving and doing a 'new thing' (new to us, not to Him) and it's unappealing or awkward, maybe even said to be 'off' from what is right. Remember, the Israelites wanted to return to their place of captivity when God was leading them into their promised land. The journey didn't look like what they expected it to, so someone must have heard incorrectly! (Tongue in cheek)

It's the lack of understanding and inability to recognize Him in what appears to be an *undone* mess, or when going in a different direction from the so-called norm when many in the Body of Christ begin to pray the soulish prayers. They are petitioning for people and ministries to be 'brought back to where they were once at'. What they don't perceive is the people aren't *off*, instead, they are finally allowing God to move them out of the box and into the liberty of the Spirit.

When the Lord was imparting this information to me, He said, *"What they are asking for is a mindset formed from a religious spirit and it is NOT My desire. If what they ask for is accomplished, disunity will prevail and My Spirit will once again be placed beneath the agenda of the flesh. That which has been called structure, is protocol."* (Structure – a construction made up of a combination of related parts. Protocol – the code and rules of diplomatic and state etiquette.)

Prior to being told about the soulish prayers, I had a dream of which the Lord quickened my remembrance to when He began to speak to me about this topic. In the dream, I was driving to a destination that I had not been to before. I needed to stop and ask directions as I was unsure of the last part of the drive. I stopped at a little house which appeared to be warm and inviting. It was lined with a white picket fence surrounding the yard. At the door, I was greeted by the sweetest little old lady, with the sweetest sounding voice. As I stood in the doorway of her house listening to the directions she was giving me, her cat kept positioning itself behind me. It was a very large black and white cat with a mouth that was so exaggeratedly widespread, it was whimsical in appearance. I was aware of this cat's purpose in staying positioned behind me was because it wanted to bite the calf of my leg. I was trying to be courteous to the woman, giving her my undivided attention as she was speaking to me, yet I knew if I didn't do something the cat would surely bite me. I turned around quickly, stomped my foot and told the cat to go away. It would back off momentarily, then would reposition itself with the same agenda.

Each time I would abruptly turn towards the cat, catching a glimpse of its opened mouth, ready to latch onto my leg. Its attempts were unsuccessful, but I'd like you to pay close attention to the next part of this dream. After several times of this occurring, the old lady said to me in the sweetest, most affectionate voice, "Oh, honey, he's only trying to pray for you."

You see, what she perceived as 'praying' for me, would have been wounding to me. The cat in the dream represents those members of the Body of Christ who are operating from a religious perspective, rather than a grace perspective. The cat was black and white because there was no middle ground to be found. In other words, it judged everyone's actions as either right or wrong, void of the grace which would cover the 'hidden truths' found within each individual circumstance. The cat trying to bite my leg while my back was turned symbolizes the backbiting in the Body, which often is disguised as, 'I'm telling you this about sister 'so&so' so we can lift her up in prayer. For the greater part, those words are used when camouflaging gossip. The old lady mentioned the cat only wanted to pray for me, but it's action was obviously going to hurt me instead of helping me. She's referring to the soulish prayers being prayed from our own agenda for others, rather than what is the Lord's will for them. The cat's mouth was exaggeratedly widespread, symbolizing how widespread it is within the Church, of those who are praying soulish prayers and exaggerating the small issues into being larger than they should be.

In our natural understanding and perspective, we are very limited. We tend to perceive through a filter which is for the most part, formed by reasons of our individual experiences and revelations. We also do not have the ability to view into a person's heart, without the Lord supernaturally giving us that revelation. Therefore, what we see outwardly is merely a small portion of a bigger story.

When we make judgments of what someone else should have done differently, or what we feel is the best solution for their life, we may be missing the mark drastically because we do not have knowledge of the entire circumstance, or simply the long-range plan of the Lord.

God has called us to be a people of love and unity and that means, there is no room for judging and condemnation among us. Does that mean we can never disagree? Certainly not. Disagreement and judging are not the same. In fact, when disagreeing in a correct manner, it should not invoke disunity at all. For example, you may think one specific model of vehicle is the best one ever made, while I think a different one is. We disagree about that matter, and yet we can both drive the vehicle of our choice to get us to the same prayer meeting. Then, I can pray for you to stop being deceived about which is the better vehicle. Just kidding…sort of.

I realize disagreeing on matters such as a vehicle of choice is insignificant, as opposed to the more heart-felt topics more likely to bring disunity. It's not my intentions to diminish the importance of such topics, rather of bringing into perspective a greater emphasis on the importance of unity, than on our disagreement. It's not our appointed position to change another person's perspective. Our position is to leave it in the hands of the Holy Spirit. In doing so, we would be allowing ourselves a much greater likelihood of walking in unity. It's a matter of choosing to focus more on the One who knitted us together as one Body, rather than the point of disagreement itself. Besides, what if we're the one who's perspective needs changed, and not the other person?

We're spirit filled beings, encased in a natural body by which we use natural senses to perceive the world around us; (sight, smell, touch, hearing, taste). With that being said, how do we go beyond our natural perception of what we hear or see, to prevent judging one another? Or, judging our circumstances wrongly? We already know that our natural perception fails us in discerning the true intent of the heart. The only way we can overcome the inclination to pass judgment using the natural appearance of people and situations, is by implementing the gift of grace we've been issued.

A few months ago, I awoke to hearing the Lord say, *"Forgive them, they know not what they do. Grace is the element for healing. Let grace arise and let grace abound. For as freely as you have been given, just as freely give."* That means with no strings attached. There were no; *if's*, *and's* or *but's*, to the grace we were given. Only a, 'receive'. As we have received, we are to also give.

'Forgive them', might apply to those we know to be in sin. It's possible, it also applies to our own inclination to pass judgment on those we 'assume' are in sin, by all natural appearances. In either case – rather than being Judge and Condemner, is it not of greater benefit to our own body to nurture and care for each fellow member?

When my finger was broken, I did not cut it off. Instead, I took exceptional care of it until it was restored. Isn't that the least we should be doing with one another? What if I had the mindset that my finger was broken and therefore was no longer as valuable to me? Due to its setback, should I no longer want it around and have no further use for it in my life? That'd be absurd, wouldn't it? My finger wasn't just sprained or jammed, the truth of the matter was, it was undoubtedly broken. Yet, I still wanted it and needed it as much as any other part of my body. Even if the truth is, one of our members is sinning, is it not much better to *lovingly* tend to them until they are restored, as opposed to cutting them off? Wouldn't each one of us want that for ourselves? I have no doubt, I would. Our instructions are to give - not as we may have received from someone else, on the contrary - as we have received from Jesus.

'Love your neighbor as you love yourself.' Matthew 22:39

In Acts 6, people were complaining because their widows were being left out of the daily distribution of food and assistance. It may have very easily appeared to them as if the disciples didn't care enough to tend to the needs of the widows. Most likely, it would be closer to the truth to say, the disciples were so busy they weren't even aware of this problem until they heard the complaints. Point being, it could have been misinterpreted that the disciples didn't care enough about these poor women to take care of their needs. Therefore, their conversations among themselves or possibly even their prayers for the disciples may have been misconstrued. The disciples weren't appointed for the distribution of food, they were called to distribute spiritual food and so was the point of their focus. When made aware of the issue at hand, they found a solution because they did indeed have concern for the needs of the widows. The outward appearance of circumstances does not always, and very rarely, depict the reality of the entire story and truth.

If we're not sure what to pray for ourselves or for someone else, instead of believing we have all the answers the best thing is to ask for protection in every area and for nothing less than the Lord's will to be done and surrender it to him. If you have a prayer language, pray in the Spirit, this ensures that we don't have our natural mind too involved and allows for it to be a pure and effective prayer for whomever it may be for.

Remember, to know Who's Spirit we're of means we do not allow ourselves to be condemning to others nor to ourselves. To do such a thing, is the same as 'calling down fire' upon someone. The Spirit we're of is all about grace. Grace for others and grace for ourselves.

Father, I thank You for uncovering and exposing to me those things that have been hidden from my understanding and have been a hindrance to me, and to others. I thank You for Your wonderful grace, by which I am forgiven. I ask, You would lead me by Your Spirit that I may pray according to Your will as I lift prayers for myself and for other people. Father, I thank You that by Your Spirit, You lead me in effective, fervent prayers that prove to be powerful. In the name of Jesus, Amen.

"The one who searches our hearts knows what the Spirit has in mind. The Spirit intercedes for God's people the way God wants him to."

Romans 8:27~God's Word Translation

CHAPTER 10

Out of the Cage of the Comfort Zone

Most everyone has dreams, ambitions or at the least some sort of bucket list. Although the number of people having any one of those lists may be rather high, it seems the count of those who follow through and pursue their aspiration is low. Why do you suppose that is? I believe the answer is found in two words; "we settle". We settle because we're told by so many different people all through our life, 'that's just how it is." We settle for the familiar, for the so-called 'norm', for the everyday and common place lifestyle and the oh-so familiar way of doing things because that's what we've seen our grandparents, our parents, neighbors, friends and co-workers doing our entire lives. In other words, we become comfortable and sedentary in the familiarity of life as we've always known it to be – aka; our comfort zone.

What we're overlooking in this idea is, living in our comfort zone so to speak, is like voluntarily living life in a comfortable little cage and never taking the opportunity to walk out the door and explore the big, wonderful and yes -unknown- world beyond our caged walls.

What if reaching our goals, desires and dreams in life were commonplace instead of far-fetched? What if being a part of miracles happening all around us and seeing the dead brought back to life were commonplace in our lives? What if hearing the voice of the Holy Spirit speak to us daily were commonplace? What if every day was fulfilling and filled with a recognizable purpose in your life? Why not? I believe the seeds of those things are living within each one of us and merely waiting on us to allow them to transition from a state of dormancy on the inside of us, into becoming our realities of life.

First, we must step out of our comfort zones and take a leap or maybe only a small baby step of faith. Whichever our level of faith moves us to do, it's equally a forward movement. Progress sometimes comes in leaps and bound, but for the most part it's made by taking one step at a time. The good news is, slow motion is better than no motion at all. Slow motion may require patience and hope, but it's still a forward movement. It's all about simply taking a step. One step at a time is how change is made and how we travel from place to place and from glory to glory.

On your journey delays will come. Don't allow those delays (what's slower than desired) to become hindrances (obstacles in the way), instead make each delay work for your benefit rather than against you. In short, keep on keeping on, there is a time and there is a way. Fear, reasoning and discouragement will give you a million reasons not to but faith will give you one reason that is greater than all the million put together. Faith will tell you to continue into the growing process. The maturing process. The refining process. The expanding of your territory, if you will.

Faith, simply put is believing in that which you cannot yet see with the natural eyes. And yet, believing in the existence of it nevertheless. Therefore, to step out in faith, it would require you to venture into an experience that is pretty much unknown to you. It may be frightening to some degree but remember, *unknown* does not necessarily mean dangerous or bad. We tend to give the unknown a bad rap in associating it with something to be feared, and that's just not accurate. In some instances, it may be true, but that's also like believing the world is flat therefore it's too dangerous to venture out into. In fact, the definition of unknown is as follows; *"not known; not within the range of one's knowledge, experience, or understanding; strange, unfamiliar. Not discovered, explored, identified, or ascertained."* (Dictionary.com)

Jesus said, *"A thief is only there to steal and kill and destroy. I came so they can have real and eternal life, more and better life than they ever dreamed of." John 10:10 (The Message)*

To me, this statement sounds like He's saying; *"I'm not here doing this so that Believers can live a life of mere mundane existence, but rather, I'm here doing this because the Father and I, want you Believers to live an incredibly blessed, happy, victorious and fulfilling life – beyond the ordinary and common!" (Taffie's translation)*

The Greek word for 'abundantly', as spoken in John 10:10 is *perissos*, (which is the word Jesus would have spoken at that time). *Perissos* means, *'superabundance, excessive, overflowing, surplus, over and above, more than enough, profuse, extraordinary, above the ordinary, more than sufficient.'* WOW! Get the picture? I'll take it! I want it – how about you? Well then, it all begins with; receive it *as truth*…. FOR YOURSELF! Believe it as to expect it…. FOR YOURSELF! If a person receives something as truth and believes it's real for their own life, they'll also live their life accordingly to that belief.

I've heard the argument that John 10:10 is about eternal life in Heaven. Well yes, it is true that Jesus came so all who come to know Him as Savior will receive the reward of Heaven when we depart our life here on earth. Not only is it referring to the final reward, also it is a gift of a transformed life in all aspects while living here on earth, right now. If we take a closer look at the discussion surrounding this verse it becomes obvious He's talking about our life here on earth. First, Jesus regards those who have come before Him – impersonating a savior, and that refers to here on earth. Secondly, He is speaking of those who enter through Him, that's referring to 'Believers' who are Believers here, while alive on earth. Then finally He says, "the thief". The thief will not be in Heaven having opportunity to steal, kill or to destroy any form of life from us. We can therefore conclude, He *is* referring to a time here on earth. Why not an abundant life? Why not live an abundant life now? Why not you? Why not me? No reason, other than that's the assignment of the enemy, to cause believers to

NOT believe. Or, to believe none of that is for now, or for you. Why is that his dirty little agenda? When we believe the abundant life is not for us, nor for now, it steals our hope and joy, it kills our dreams and aspirations, and destroys our faith keeping us from the 'more abundant live' Jesus came to give us.

One of the subtler and yet as I see it, more effective tactics the thief uses against us is the, "I can't" strategy. We lose out way too often because of our repetitive, 'I can't' declarations over our lives. Think about how often the 'I can't' infiltrates our lives to keep us from the best of the best for us.

- I can't afford to take a day off to enjoy time with my family;

- I can't save any money;

- I can't forgive that person;

- I can't pursue my dream;

- I can't get over this sickness;

- I can't lose weight;

- I can't find the time;

- I CAN'T, I CAN'T I CAN'T!!!

Why not? Maybe if we get down to the nitty gritty of it, much of the time what we really mean is, 'I won't'. '*I won't because I don't want to put the effort into what it will take to accomplish that dream.*' There's a difference between being cautious and complacent. Cautious allows forward movement, although it may be slow, it's still a forward progression. Whereas complacency brings everything to a standstill. I've seen too many people with regrets once they've realized what they've missed out on due to their complacency. The guarantee of complacency is lack; lack in finances, lack in relationships, lack in good health, lack of accomplishments. On the other hand, success is found in the investment of time and effort. Don't allow complacency to be a thief in your life.

The first step is always the hardest and is also the step the enemy would love nothing more than to scare us into not taking. The truth of the matter is, it scares the enemy to think of us stepping into the fullness of our destinies. It very well should!

We all too often lean on the 'I can't's', not realizing those words are a free gift from the enemy of our soul. The better choice would be, moving forward into the free gift of abundant life, from the Lover of our soul who gave His life for us.

Consider this, our Father God is perfect in all His ways and He loves us with a perfect love. Many of us are parents and although we love our children, we have not yet entered being a perfect parent nor loving with a perfected love. Even so, what parent would bring their baby into this world with merely desiring them to serve in life and not be as happy as possible nor prosper abundantly? I'm sure there are those who exist, who don't care about those issues for their children, but I guarantee they are few and far between. My point being, how much more would God, who is perfect in love and in all His ways, want all of that and still so much more for His children?

If we're being transparent, and we are, the ugly truth is if we keep trusting in the promptings of the thief, then he's correct, 'I can't'. Or, if we try to do much of anything by our own strength, well then, 'I can't' might be accurate as well. On the other hand, here's the beautiful truth, we are not our own because we've been bought with a price. The thief has no right to us nor do we need to do anything by our own strength because the Holy Spirit lives within us and we have His strength and His guidance in everything.

I'm reminded of a time when I worked in a very physically demanding factory. The work at times was hard and oftentimes we were required to not only work very quickly, but also to repeatedly lift heavy parts at the same time. This one particular time I'm reminded of, I was trying to raise the bars of a metal rack that was not seeming to budge by the efforts of my girlie muscle strength. I had been tugging from about every angle I could maneuver myself into, trying to get that rack opened. Finally, suddenly it popped up and I thought 'Aha, I did it!". When I turned around there was a man standing directly behind me. This man had seen me struggling to lift the bars and came over behind me unbeknown to me, took ahold of the rack and lifted it from behind and out of my view. After I had discovered his unseen assistance from behind me, I shared with him, I thought I did it on my own until I turned around. We both had a little chuckle over the situation. I was so very grateful he had seen my struggle and came to my rescue. It made me think about how often the Lord has our back, lifting our burdens, even in the times we're unaware of His presence.

Let this be your guiding truth, *"So, what do you think? With God on our side like this, how can we lose?"* Romans 8:31
and;
Philippians 4:13 "Whatever I have, wherever I am, I can make it through anything in the One who makes me who I am."
(The Message)

Go for those dreams and aspirations He has placed within you. The very God who gave you the breath of life also gave you hopes, dreams, gifts and talents for a purpose-filled and more abundant life, for right here right now – FOR SUCH A TIME AS THIS! Today is the day! Life is too short to always be waiting in the wings. Much too often we spend our God-given time waiting for something to happen, waiting for this and that before we step into anything of life too deeply. It seems everyone is always waiting for more money, more time, or the right moment. The truth is; we're always going to find a reason to need more money, time IS short, and there's no time like the present because tomorrow isn't guaranteed. What happened to knowing, 'time is of the essence'? We've been given an allotted amount of time to live, breathe, create and experience life to the fullest, so how about we live it out passionately?! Do the best you can NOW to enjoy the money you're working for, make the most of the time you've been given and make it the "right" moment now. When opportunity arises, whether it be for your career or recreation don't waste it away with excuses, because life is happening NOW!

We've been given the gift of 'life abundantly', let's not waste it. Live it out with joy, knowing we've been given the right to live it accordingly; live it contagiously so that the essence of who we are radiates LIFE to all who we cross paths with.

Jesus said, *"Follow me, and let the dead bury their own dead."* *Matthew 8:22 (God's Word Translation)* Let's live with intention!

God does nothing for selfish ambitions and I assure you, every dream and gift He has placed within you has a greater purpose beyond only your personal benefit. He's a god of sharing and giving as well as reaping and reward. You not only have an abundant life to live out, you also have an abundance to give out! Please don't settle for mere existence when there's so much more awaiting you. Choose life! Choose abundant life.

"This cannot be done by men. But with God all things can be done."

Matthew 19:26~New Life Version

CHAPTER 11

Moving the Mountains

I personally do not know many if anyone who instantly manifested a mature, unshakable faith from the moment they became a born-again believer. Although there are those few who walk in such a gift of faith, for the majority we must endure a process of growth and times of our faith being tried so we will be strengthened and developed into a position of maturity.

"It's impossible to please God apart from faith. And why? Because anyone who wants to approach God must believe both that he exists and that he cares enough to respond to those who seek him."
Hebrews 11:6 (The Message)

God knows exactly what it takes for each of us, as unique and individual as we are, to get us to a place of walking the walk of unshakable faith. He will allow us to go through different and unique circumstances and processes for faith to be established within us solidly.

"That's why we can be so sure that every detail in our lives of love for God is worked into something good."
Romans 8:28 (The Message)

God is calling us into a place of walking as mature sons and daughters because He is establishing His kingdom within us as it has never been.

"What is faith? It is the confident assurance that something we want is going to happen. It is the certainty that what we hope for is waiting for us, even though we cannot see it up ahead. Men of God in days of old were famous for their faith. By faith—by believing God— we know that the world and the stars—in fact, all things—were made at God's command; and that they were all made from things that can't be seen." Hebrews 11:1-3 (Living Bible)

When we see through eyes of faith our visual perception changes. Our vision is no longer zoomed in and focused on the trial, instead it is on the promise and reward to come. The exercising of our faith that occurs during a trial produces the vision that allows us to see beyond our present circumstances and farther than the here and now into the promises from our Father.

"Dear brothers and sisters, when troubles of any kind come your way, consider it an opportunity for great joy.   For you know that when your faith is tested, your endurance has a chance to grow. So, let it grow, for when your endurance is fully developed, you will be perfect and complete, needing nothing." James 1:2-4
(New Living Translation)

Please understand, no one is saying to take joy in the trial itself or to thank God that this unpleasant situation has come upon you. What it is saying, is to be thankful to God for leading you through the trial and rejoice for the harvest that's awaiting on the other side of it. You see, it's when we look up from our place of tribulation and choose to see farther with a faith inspired vision that mountains are moved and we can praise our way right through and out of the prison of circumstances.

I pray (literally, I am praying for you as I type this) you get the vision of the promise of the Lord for you in your life. Stand solidly on the words He's spoken to you, whether they be the written word of God or the rhema word of God and let those promises be your undying testimony. Speak them over and over, however many times it's necessary for you to do it until you truly have them written on your heart as absolute truth.

Say them aloud. *"So, then faith comes by hearing, and hearing by the word of God." Romans 10:17 (NKJV)*

For every situation in your life that is opposing God's promises for you, speak boldly the truth of His word into those areas of your life. Command them to align with the will of our Father in Heaven. Let faith be aroused in you that you may see clearly your place of trial is only for a moment of time. In that faith, let your praises ring out and take up the authority given to you in the name of Jesus, our Lord. God never fails us or falls short, and He is for us!

While I was praying for the healing of a dear friend, I heard the words, *"It's hammer time!"*. About a week prior, a television program happened to catch my attention when someone said the phrase, "it's hammer time". They then proceeded to do a dance in reference to the rapper M.C. Hammer. With that in mind I thought, "hammer time"? So, I quickly tried to push those words aside. Again, except this time a little stronger and more firmly I heard the words, "it's hammer time!" Okay, now there is no doubt that I'm not recalling some secular catch phrase. The Lord was speaking to me and I needed to listen up. The Holy Spirit then began to stir within me the revelation of what He meant in that repeated phrase. Although, the world's notion of hammer time involves rapping to some music, God's idea of it takes on a totally different meaning. God was saying, it's time to *rap* the heads of our enemies into fine powder with the hammer of His word and the power of His Holy Spirit within us.

Per the definition in Webster's dictionary, 'rap' means: *"To strike with a quick, smart blow or blows. Or, to utter suddenly and forcibly; to deliver with a bang.*

God said to me, *"When the enemy tries to take a stand against you, do not hesitate, strike him quickly with the hammer of My word, take back all that was taken and move on without breaking your stride."*

It seems to me that the Lord is directing us to speak His word so swiftly and with such power that we will be far ahead of the enemy before he even realizes what hit him. God gave us dominion. We may have let it slip out of our stewardship for a time but hear me now, the awakening is here and it's time to take back from the enemy all that belongs to us. Through Jesus He's given us the authority, the legal right, the power and every weapon needed to get the job done. He's given us the name of Jesus – the name above all names by which every knee will bow down to. In His name, we are to walk in His authority. Webster defines 'authority' as such; *"Legal or rightful power; a right to command or to act"*. Jesus has not given us His authority that we *might* walk in it - *just in case* we really get desperate - or for selfish gain. Walking in His authority is more than just a right that has been given to us. Because He has given us free will, we do have the choice to take it or leave it, but if we desire to be faithful stewards in His kingdom we should not even consider walking in His authority as being an option. His authority has been given to us to walk in as a part of our daily life.

"My coming can be compared with that of a man who went on a trip to another country. He laid out his employees' work for them to do while he was gone and told the gatekeeper to watch for his return." Mark 13:34 (Living Bible)

As joint heirs with Christ we have a *responsibility* to walk in His authority, taking back the dominion while here on earth. Walking in His authority goes hand in hand with being a good steward of the kingdom.

He has given us the power of His Spirit that we may speak His word with authority to reveal His truth and good news of salvation, in order to; break off strongholds of bondages, heal sicknesses and diseases, overcome poverty, and to set free those who are tormented by demons. The Lord told me, *"This is not a time of grueling warfare, this is a time of refreshing."* How refreshing it is, to have all that our Father has given to us through Jesus, and to live truly as who He created us to be. The Lord has prepared the way before us and become as a shield behind us, so let's take back the authority. When we believe God's word and declare it accordingly, we will then see changes in the circumstances of our lives that do not line up with His word.

A few days after the Lord had spoken to me about 'hammer time', a friend called me, distressed over ground (spiritually speaking) that had obviously been stolen by the enemy. I shared with her what the Lord had spoken to me about hammer time and told her to bang the enemy's head (head = authority) with the Word and tell him to give back what he stole. We hung up the phone and she hammered the enemy with the word of God. By that night, the ground that had been stolen was restored.

When we speak the word of God, we can and should expect to see the confirming signs following.

Speaking the word + expectant faith = mountain moving results!

The Lord shared with me once, the one thing the enemy fears greatly is that we will come to realize he fears us – knowing the authority we've been given. If we don't recognize what we have then we won't walk in it and the enemy has nothing to fear. But, if we know we have it and walk in it, that's what makes him tremble in fear because he knows his deceptions have no power over us.

Does not my word burn like fire? asks the Lord. Is it not like a mighty hammer that smashed the rock to pieces? Jeremiah 23:29 (Living Bible)

Awhile back the Lord told me it's time for His people to stop following behind Him and begin to follow *alongside* of Him. He's calling forth His people to be as mature sons and daughters that will co-labor with Him. As it says in 2 Corinthians 5:20, we're called to be ambassadors for Christ. The word ambassador comes from the root word, *'presbeuo' (pres-byoo-oh)* meaning *'to be elder' – a representative of one who is a ruling authority.* A look at a little history of ambassadors would tell us the ambassadors would be chosen from the ranks of mature, experienced men. To be an ambassador for Christ requires one to walk in spiritual maturity. Scripturally speaking, one who is mature is one who is solid in knowing who they are in Christ and unwaveringly understands and believes the word of God.

The Lord went on to also tell me, *"My Spirit is sweet and fragrant and is ready to be poured out upon the earth as that of fine, rare and highly valued and sought after, fragrant oil.* (As He spoke this to me, the room filled with His fragrance – as that of a sweet-smelling perfume.) *Come up here, co-labor beside Me, not behind Me. It is time for your every step to be in step with My every step."*

"Jesus called his twelve disciples together and gave them authority to drive out evil spirits and to heal every disease and every sickness." Matthew 10:1 (Good News Translation)

Jesus gave power to His disciples! The word 'disciple' comes from the Greek word *'mathetes' (math-ay-tace)* which in turn comes from the verb *'manthano'*. Manthano's root word is 'math' – a word suggesting, *'thought with effort put forth'*. That means you put some action to your thoughts. To have a thought without an action coming as a direct result from it can be likened to James 2:17 wherein it says, *"faith without works is dead"*. Just as faith merits action, there must also be an action stemming from a thought for it to become alive and productive.

A disciple is a learner which is, one who follows both the teaching and the teacher but not in thought only. A disciple follows with effort put forth, thus resulting in a disciple being one who is an active participant.

"And those who believe shall use my authority to cast out demons, and they shall speak new languages. They will be able even to handle snakes with safety, and if they drink anything poisonous, it won't hurt them; and they will be able to place their hands on the sick and heal them." Mark 16:17-18 (The Message)

We quote this scripture frequently, but do we really understand what it means to believe? The word, 'believe', comes from the Greek word *'pisteus' (pist-yoo-oh)* which means, *to trust in, have faith in, be fully convinced of, acknowledge, rely on.* In other words, it's what we know to be so true we act upon it without the presence of doubt. Actions prove belief! You have heard the saying, 'Actions speak louder than words' – it can be very true. Our words are powerful and have the authority to change the course of situations, but if we do not have the faith to put action to our words then our words are simply in vain.

If we say we love someone but all the while behaving in a manner which is cruel and wicked to them, our words of love are empty. Our actions have not brought our words into an agreement to affirm one another. Likewise, faith will produce the behavior reflecting faith.

When we truly believe what we say, then we also *'do'* as we say. Our belief spurs faith to act upon that belief, regardless of what the circumstances around us appear to be. Having faith means we don't require proof *prior* to our actions. As we stand in faith on the word of God, declaring it without doubt, we can expect evidence to be produced *because* of our faith and His faithfulness combined. It's pleasing to God when we approach Him in faith because His desire is to reward us and faith is the open door by which the reward it delivered through. Faith is also the staple ingredient for us to live a victorious life as an overcomer. The Lord already cleared the way before us, now the only thing we need to do is simply and unwaveringly believe Him at His word.

"Look, I have given you authority over all the power of the enemy, and you can walk among snakes and scorpions and crush them. Nothing will injure you." Luke 10:19 (New Living Translation)

In case that one line didn't jump out at you, let me place an emphasis on it…, *"over ALL the power of the enemy"*! We've been given authority over who? The enemy! Does the enemy have power? Sure, but it doesn't stand up to the power the Lord holds. Jesus has authority over ALL the power of the enemy and He has imparted it to us!! Through Jesus we have been given authority over anything the enemy would try to come against us with. Anything! Everything!

The word *authority* means, *legal or rightful power, a right to command or to act.* When we sincerely grasp 'with understanding, unto believing' the demonic is more fearful of us because of WHO is within us, that's when we'll walk in the authority and power we've been given. This is the indisputable truth; when we speak the word of God believing Him at His word, the demons and anything that does not line up with the will of God must submit. If you don't see the submission the first time you take authority and speak to the mountain, then do it again, and do it again, and again if necessary. Do it until your breakthrough comes. If at first you don't 'see' your success, try and try again until it manifests into view.

His power is alive and flowing through us and once you receive the breakthrough in one area, your faith will become stronger and you will find you have faith to move mountains that are a little larger than what the last ones were. Grasping the understanding unto believing means the word no longer remains as only head knowledge but has now become written on the tablets of your heart rather than merely the book you're reading from.

The Lord has already provided us with everything we will ever need; deliverance, healing, provision, protection, wisdom – we need only to believe Him for it. (Matthew 6)

The enemy's goal is to make sure we come into agreement with every bit of doubt and fear he can use for intimidation to result in us being overcome instead of being the OVERCOMERS! He can only be successful if we allow him to be, and when we place our focus on ourselves and our circumstances instead of looking to the Lord and His report, that's when we become intimidated. When discouragement sets in, that marks the onslaught of believing the lies of the enemy and the battle begins to take on the appearance of hopelessness. The Lord once told me my greatest enemy was discouragement. When we make a place of agreement with discouragement we tend to soon-there-after, give up. As Believers, we must see the enemy as he really is – beneath our feet!

Jesus said *in Matthew 16:19 "I will give you the keys (authority) of the kingdom of heaven; and whatever you bind [forbid, declare to be improper and unlawful] on earth will have [already] been bound in heaven, and whatever you loose [permit, declare lawful] on earth will have [already] been loosed in heaven." (Amplified Bible)*

How amazing is that? We've been given the authority to bind up that which opposes the will of God and, to loose His promises – not only in our own lives but also in the lives of others!

We may be in warfare, but the warfare is no longer to be a warfare of travail and feeling the pressure of grueling war. It's a warfare that is fought in the celebration of praising Jesus Christ and in the authority of speaking His word in the confident faith that moves mountains. Our warfare is victorious because our rejoicing and celebration isn't found within our authority, it's found within our names being written in the Lamb's Book of Life. Otherwise, we would only have reason to rejoice during our times of 'seeing' victory. With our rejoicing being in our salvation, there's no ceasing of it.

"You don't have enough faith," Jesus told them. "I tell you the truth, if you had faith even as small as a mustard seed, you could say to this mountain, 'Move from here to there,' and it would move. Nothing would be impossible. Matthew 17:20 (New Living Translation)

"The sound of declaration, praise and worship that goes out from you in the natural may not sound to you as a fierce weapon of warfare – or as if penetrating into the realms of the supernatural, nor may it seem to you very powerful to your natural sense of hearing. Even so, be of no doubt, within the spiritual realm where authority is recognized and faith is the loudest, the fiercest and effectively penetrating sound of all, your words of declaration, your praise in the face of trials and your sweet, most holy form of worship – (that which is from your heart) – echoes; pierces and shakes through the heavenlies with the greatest, most beautiful and powerful force of sound that does more than you can see or hear with the natural perceptions. Therefore, don't doubt

yourself. Don't doubt the sound of your voice. Don't doubt the effectiveness of your praise, or the beauty of your praises. Do not doubt the depth of your worship. So often you struggle with 'feeling' your measure of worship is shallow, merely because you do not 'feel' it going into the depths you desire to 'feel'. Do you not know that the Spirit of the Living God is within you and goes forth, being manifested into the atmosphere within each and every one of those displays of your heart and voice? Yes, up from your heart, and out through your voice – yes, YOUR VOICE! The enemy would like nothing more than for you to doubt the beauty, effectiveness and power of your own voice. Why? Because when you release your words/voice in faith – even in the smallest amount of faith, it renders his plans ineffective. Release the sound of your voice confidently, knowing you are the Holy Spirit's mouthpiece." (spoken to me by Holy Spirit)

When we speak negative words about our situation or grumble about what we 'see' as our present so-called 'reality', we are speaking (declaring) the troubles and problems over and over. In so doing, we're reinforcing them to be more solidly established. It's very much like handing the enemy bullets in which he uses to fight against us with. Disarming the enemy is a better solution to a faster victory!

"I have given you hope and victory through My words of promise and life. Speaking words that declare My goodness and faithfulness into your situations (regardless of how dire your battles may see or feel in the heat of the moment) is steadily disarming the enemy at the frontlines." (spoken to me by the Holy Spirit)

At times in our lives it may seem questionable, especially in the most unbearable heat of the fire, but undoubtedly God knows exactly what it takes for each of us, to ensure we get to an unshakable faith. HE will allow us to go through different and unique circumstances and processes for our faith to be established within us solidly. Although it appears to be quite the opposite the time during the 'dark night of our soul' is most likely the very hour the victory for our promises is established.

"That afternoon, the whole earth was covered with darkness for three hours, from noon until three o'clock. About three o'clock, Jesus shouted, "Eli, Eli, lama sabachthani?" which means, "My God, my God, why have you forsaken me?" Matthew 27:45-46 (Living Bible)

At first thought it may not always seem like a loving Father to allow us to endure hardships but I assure you, it most certainly is. If a parent saw their baby was about to try taking the first step and were to repeatedly pick him/her up in fear he might fall, how would the infant ever learn to walk on its own? Sure, the young child would never get hurt from a fall but also would never develop leg muscle strong enough to carry its own weight very far, nor the understanding of how to balance on his legs. The result would be a person who is forever dependent on someone else or on an external device to move them from place to place, even so much as within their own home. Would it sincerely be an *act of love* to run to the infant's rescue as to prevent those small falls, or is the continual running to the rescue caused by the presence of fear? A loving parent understands the small amount of pain ensued by falling the short distance is quite insignificant in comparison to the reward of the accomplishment.

Too often we assume God is the creator of every trial or hardship we find ourselves involved in. Therefore, we also may want to blame God because of that manner of thinking. Our trials are formed by a variety of sources. Sometimes they are the consequences of the choices we've made. Simple as that. If you choose to kick a boulder while barefoot, don't blame God for the broken toes you now must deal with! I know it sounds ridiculous but people make foolish choices all the time, then want to blame God for the adverse consequences they must endure as a result.

Some of our trials may very well be concocted for us by our enemy for a plan to cause harm to us in one way or another. All in all, it doesn't really matter by what means the trial was brought to us. If we put our faith in God, while He may not have created the trial, He will certainly be the director of our steps through it. Although He permits us to walk through hard times, you can take confidence in knowing He has a plan - not to crush you, rather to season and to prosper you. For the sake of clarity, there is a difference between creating and allowing something. More often than not, we are our own creators of our consequences of which God allows us to walk through. In the process, we are learning and growing in wisdom, hopefully in knowledge as well, to not recreate the situation again.

You see, when that baby is taking those first steps, he is very wobbly, uncertain of how to move one foot in front of the other and unstable. His time falling is more than his time spent taking steps. After a while he begins to develop the skill to steady himself and he finds his balance little by little. Before long, he's trotting from room to room, quite confident and fearless in the journey with much less falling down time than time spent upright.

Just as with the depiction of the toddler learning to walk confidently and unshakably, we too are learning to be stable, unshakable and mature in our faith so that we also will soon be overcoming anything and everything that would attempt to slow us down or hinder our stride in anyway.

As we are becoming transformed into those unshakable people, you may be finding you must endure fiery trials in your life. Trials are never pleasant, regardless they are the necessary training ground for us. It may not be until the close of the trial we're walking through, we realize faith is in fact being built and strengthened within us. Does not discouragement come because for the most part we view our trials as a waste of time and as a setback in our progression? If we can recognize while yet in our place of trial, patience is being produced within us and we are being made mature in character then we will be more equipped to rejoice for the reward awaiting us.

By the way, never underestimate the power of being patient. Within patience is self-discipline, wisdom, and peace. Patience deters us from making quick and foolish decisions. Patience is a power within itself, if you will. It is indeed a virtue.

We want to be mountain moving people. We need to be. God wants us to be. The mountains are those things which come to hinder us and to stand in the way of us receiving the promises of the Lord. His promises are the blessings, healing, rest and peace, financial prosperity, and abundant life! Think about being on a journey, you look up and there stands a big ole mountain right in your path. You look around and there's no other way to get to where you're going other than straight ahead. The problem is, there's this mountain in front of you and it's not going anywhere. The journey looks grim. What now? Good question and one that should be answered by the Lord.

"When the disciples had Jesus off to themselves, they asked, "Why couldn't we throw it out?" Because you're not yet taking God seriously," said Jesus. "The simple truth is that if you had a mere kernel of faith, a poppy seed, say, you would tell this mountain, 'Move!' and it would move. There is nothing you wouldn't be able to tackle."
Matthew 17:19-20 (The Message)

It is impossible to move mountains without the presence of faith. Mountain moving faith really is attained by the ability to see the promises/rewards to come as more of a reality than what the troubles of today are.

Those things which are in opposition to the word of God, (whether it be the written word, or the words He has spoken into your heart for your life) are only temporal are not God's truth. They may seem to be 'in your face', and aggressive for a time, but they will pass away because they cannot remain in existence as you speak and stand in faith on His word.

God NEVER fails us or falls short and He IS for us!

"So, we're not giving up. How could we! Even though on the outside it often looks like things are falling apart on us, on the inside, where God is making new life, not a day goes by without his unfolding grace. These hard times are small potatoes compared to the coming good times, the lavish celebration prepared for us. There's far more here than meets the eye. The things we see now are here today, gone tomorrow. But the things we can't see now will last forever."

2 Corinthians 4:16-18 ~ The Message

CHAPTER 12

Building Upon Truth or Facts?

My son and his wife had a dog given to them due to an unfortunate event of circumstances happening in the previous owner's life. The dog seemed like a well-trained pet and was quite the beauty. As anyone would be to have such a pet given to them, they were delighted to receive him into their household.

As it turned out, a few of the vital details about this beauty of a dog were left unmentioned prior to acceptance of him. For instance, he had a phobia with being left alone. This dog was a good-sized fella and quite strong as well, which presented the problem of him having the strength needed, allowing him to bust out of the crates they attempted to secure him while they were out of the house. He also had the ability to tear up the doors that stood as a barrier between him and his people. Obviously, due to the dog's large size, strength and separation anxiety, it would take special accommodations to secure this guy properly, of which they were unprepared to supply. Given the circumstances, they were discussing the options of relocating the dog to a home offering better provision for him. Keep in mind, this knowledge is now stored within my brain-bank of information.

Meanwhile, my other son and I took our dog to his vet appointment. We were sitting in the reception area waiting for our turn when a woman with her dog entered the front of the room. She stood with her dog, waiting for service at the receptionist desk. I began noticing the dog and how much it resembled my other son's dog. I began questioning in my mind if that could possibly be his dog. Surely not.

Possibly? It looked almost identical to his dog but what are the chances? On that note, I decided to snap a picture of the dog, thinking I might send it to my son to show him how much this other dog looked like his. The resemblance was uncanny.

Now, here's where the story takes a surprise twist. When the receptionist greeted the woman, the woman with the dog said to the receptionist, "I'm here with (the name of the dog) for his appointment." What??? That's my son's dog's name! It is him! So now I'm studying every detail of this dog even more closely! Same appearance, same name, even the same collar! I motioned to gain my other son's attention for him to also take note of this dog. He confirmed, it seemed to be his brother's dog.

Now it was quite the coincidence that the new owner brought the dog into the vet while my son and I happened to be there but it gave me a sense of relief to see they had obviously found a new home for their dog.

My son who owned the dog, was at work that day so I thought I'd go ahead and send the picture of his former dog with a text saying, "hey, look who showed up at the vet while we were there!" To my surprise, after he received the photo he began asking a series of questions as to why the dog was there with someone else, and so on. Neither he nor his wife had given the dog away, and neither one of them were at home that day.

Was it possible someone who may have known they wanted to find it a new home, took the dog in their absence? Had someone stolen the dog? Assumptions and various scenarios were running rampant through all our thoughts, to say the least! Cutting through the chase, we made the decision to stop by my son's house on our way home with the intent of verifying the dog's whereabouts, or in this case – MIA status. I arrived at my son's house to find – low and behold – his dog was still there safe and sound. No way! Oooh...but yes...yes indeed he was there.

By all appearances, everything lined up in such a way it made it super easy to assume those two dogs were one in the same. They looked identical, they wore the same collar, and how crazy is this? – they even had the same name! All the facts were in place, but the truth and the story told by the facts along with assumption, were not the same. They were not the same dog at all. The facts created an illusion of two completely different dogs appearing to be only one. Without the presence of truth, facts do not necessarily create a valid foundation. A conclusion based on mere facts alone *can be* nothing more than assumptions placed between each fact, in an attempt to bond them together to form a completion. Without knowledge of actual truths, this can be way off base, as it was with the dog.

We passed judgment by means of appearance of the situation and assumed by weighing in all the facts, our final judgment was truth. According to our analysis of the facts, someone else had taken their dog without their knowledge. Sure, the facts were there right before our eyes. We could see them as plain as day, but truth did not rest within the facts of what we could visibly see. Our natural vision gave us the facts before us, and our logical mind converted that into what was truth in relation to what we believed we saw. It was a very deceiving situation, our eyes told us one thing, but the truth was something different.

In the bible, we read we're not to go by our natural eyesight alone but to walk by faith. We're to walk in a greater depth of the spirit man than what we allow the natural man to rule over us. Our natural man was born into a deceptive world, in a deceptive flesh, that if not ruled over can be deceiving to the perception of reality.

How many times have we thought we've seen one thing, only to find out our eyes have played tricks on us? Or how many times have our thoughts gone in the wrong direction and we had a circumstance totally misunderstood? Have you ever heard the lyrics to a song incorrectly and thought for a while the singer was saying one thing to discover later, you had been singing the wrong lyrics for the last two months? I have! Sometimes, those scenarios can be quite amusing and we get a good laugh out of them. In those instances, the misinterpretation is harmless but what about the times when misinterpreting the facts can cause damage. If we, by way of natural perception fail to realize truth over what we see as facts, we're doing nothing more than building upon a false foundation.

"When the servant of the man of God got up in the morning and went outside, he saw troops, horses, and chariots surrounding the city. Elisha's servant asked, "Master, what should we do?" Elisha answered, "Don't be afraid. We have more forces on our side than they have on theirs." Then Elisha prayed, "Lord, please open his eyes so that he may see." The Lord opened the servant's eyes and let him see. The mountain around Elisha was full of fiery horses and chariots." 2 Kings 6:15-17 (GOD'S WORD Translation)

When the servant judged the situation by what he could visibly see before him, his conclusion was that of failure for the battle they were about to face. When God allowed him to see truth beyond the natural facts presented before him, he then saw a totally opposite perspective. He no longer saw defeat, he saw VICTORY!

We've all heard the saying, 'don't judge a book by its cover', not only is there wisdom in that, it lines up with scripture. When we judge a book by what we see on the outside, we decide immediately whether that book's contents are interesting and worth reading or not. In other words, we don't give it a fair nor genuine chance. We look at it and draw our conclusion entirely by what we see on the outside without knowing in the least bit, the wealth of knowledge and depth of information it may be hiding within its core. God instructs us not to judge because we look upon the outward man, and cast our judgment on what we 'view' as to be factual.

On the other hand, God being the only one who can see the true heart of a person along with every thought and intention within circumstances, He alone judges purely and righteously.

It might seem to you a bit trivial that I wrongly judged in my conclusion about the dog but it was a powerful lesson for me to learn. I had a hands-on crash course, if you will. The most memorable lessons are the ones we walk through rather than simply read about. Thankfully, in this instance it was a dog and not a person. Experiencing this in the way I did was not only an eye opener for me in a sense but it also showed me in our humanness, how easily we misjudge one another. Not necessarily because of ill intentions to hurt one another, instead, simply because of human error.

Some years ago, I experienced this same type of judgement on the other side of the fence. I was wrongly judged based on the appearance of a situation I was walking through in my life at that time. To have many of my fellow believers accept what they perceived as truth based on the appearance of my circumstances, was honestly, the most devastating and hurtful time throughout my entire life (up to this point).

Why was that so devastating to me, or for that matter, to any other person who has had the same experience? When we accuse, judge or assume wrongly with one another, we're wounding a vital part of our own body. As the Body of Christ, we're one in Him. We're all extensions of the same body, with Christ as our Head. Therefore, it goes to say, we are called to walk in unity and oneness with each other. Accusations and judgements break the flow of unity by causing wounds, suspicion, mistrust and oftentimes, shame. All those things hinder us from being truly unified.

Keep in mind, various circumstances can form and shape the appearance of a situation both positively and negatively. Nevertheless, that does not mean the heart of a situation is as such as what the appearance suggests it to be. Judging by the outward appearance, we may believe certain people are wealthy when they are struggling to pay their bills. We don't see that part of their lives so we draw our conclusions based on their nice clothes, houses and cars they have. I know of a man who lives in an old shack of a house, dirty and filled with trash. He never looks clean or well dressed and by all appearances if one didn't know otherwise, you could easily conclude he is very poor. The truth is, he is financially well-off. His appearance gives the impression he is poor but the truth is, he saves his money and refuses to spend it on anything other than his very minimal and basic needs. His bank account speaks quite an opposite truth as to what his appearance does. Remember, when we draw conclusions based on facts and not truth we are establishing judgment on a false foundation.

We probably all know couples who seem to be happily married but hear stories from them in regard to what takes place behind closed doors. We may see smiles and believe they are the picture-perfect image of what marriage should be, while in secret there is abuse taking place.

There could be times you might drive past our house and the fact is, there's someone else's vehicle parked in our driveway. You might then go tell a mutual friend you would have stopped to visit me but I already had company, so you drove on. The fact would be, yes there was a vehicle parked in our driveway that didn't belong to us, but the truth is, we share a driveway with our neighbor so they may have had company and not us.

I'm almost one-hundred percent positive, in the hours Jesus was hanging on the cross it appeared to be anything except victorious. The facts were, He was beaten and put to death. The truth was, He was victorious and conquered death!

Just as it is important that we not judge one another because we cannot discern the heart of a person, it is also important to be careful not to misjudge circumstances by appearance only. It's possible that we can judge our circumstances by what they look like outwardly, all the while, cursing them with our negative words and opinions. Such actions and misjudgments on our behalf causes us to miss the true intent and transitions those very circumstances are providing via the unseen. Patience is particularly important, when waiting on our circumstances to show their true colors. They may at first appear black as the middle of night, but in time, we see the brightness of their developing colors shining forth and realize it merely took a little time in the process.

Whether we're speaking of people or our circumstances, it's best to ask the Lord what He sees as opposed to us declaring and speaking what we see through a natural perception which can be very flawed and weak. The Spirit knows and makes known.

"But the LORD told Samuel, "Don't look at his appearance or how tall he is, because I have rejected him. God does not see as humans see. Humans look at outward appearances, but the LORD looks into the heart."

1 Samuel 16:7~God's Word Translation

CHAPTER 13

Body + Mind + Spirit = Whole Person

I'm a contemplative person and in so being I often ponder life, love, truth, relationships, what many consider to be happiness and that's just my brief list of contemplatives. What I'm writing comes from the pondering and in the seeking of the Holy Spirit from within my heart and the conclusions from my own life experiences. I'm sharing them with you for the possibility that in something of them you might find a small portion of direction for yourself, hope, or some form of revelation that may help in your own journey in life.

There are many things we pursue in our endeavor of trying to find the key to happiness, and what we believe to be success; fame, beauty, higher education, the perfect career, financial wealth, popularity, romance, material possessions, etc. None of those things are wrong in themselves, and each one may very well be a contribution into our lives that brings some satisfaction. Ultimately, true happiness can't come without first having peace, which comes by way of spiritual reconciliation unto God through Jesus.

> "Jesus answered him, "I am the way, the truth, and the life. No one goes to the Father except through Me." John 14:6
> (GOD'S WORD Translation)

Given, without this reconciliation there is a void within. Let me further say, being created human we also have been created with not only a spiritual need but a human/flesh need and desire, as well. For example, 'man cannot live on bread alone but from every word that proceeds from the mouth of the Lord'. (Deut. 8:3) That verse is addressing not to only nourish our natural/human person that we are but also make sure our spirits within are being nourished. We are a multifaceted creation. Not only are we consisting of human flesh but also, we are spirit. We are not intended to nourish the one and neglect the other for we are an entire package of flesh (body), spirit and soul (mind).

"Suppose a believer, whether a man or a woman, needs clothes or food and one of you tells that person, "God be with you! Stay warm, and make sure you eat enough." If you don't provide for that person's physical needs, what good does it do?" James 2:15-16 (GOD'S WORD Translation)

Too often, the church, the religious community, Believers, whatever you want to refer to us as, have neglected the truth that we were created as human beings with certain wants, desires and needs which are perfectly normal and right. There is nothing out of bounds to want a career or to enjoy some of the finer things in life, and therefore we should not be shamed nor shaming others for enjoying any one of those things. There's nothing wrong with wanting to look good and take care of yourself. It's a good thing to pursue a college degree and higher education. Money is a blessing and can be used to do incredible things for the needs of others and even simply some of our own needs and 'wants'. Desiring to have companionship is not wrong and shouldn't be labeled as such. Any one of those things (but not limited to them) only become out of balance when they are being pursued *above* our relationship with Christ or when we become entirely focused on them, they begin to hinder our walk with Him.

The truth is, we were created to love and be loved, not just knowing the love of our Creator but also to know love and companionship of romance, friendship and family. One of the greatest afflictions in the pursuit of happiness is knowing the sorrow of rejection and lost love. I'm sorry, we're fooling ourselves if we pretend we really don't need or want anyone else other than a relationship with Jesus. Now, I know there are those who are called to a life of never marrying and living a total surrender to the Lord. That's an amazing gift of grace those people have been given to live that type of life out and be at peace with it. Seriously, they are few and far between.

Now the Lord God said, "It is not good (beneficial) for the man to be alone; I will make him a helper [one who balances him—a counterpart who is] suitable and complementary for him."
Genesis 2:18 (Amplified Bible)

You see, it was God's conclusion people need companionship, love *and* romance. Keep in mind, He did not decide this *after* sin crept into the garden. Nope! He made the decision that people need companionship other than Him, while He was still walking in the garden daily with His creation. If you don't believe God designed us with the need and desire for passionate love and romance, read the Song of Solomon. He most certainly did!

Song of Solomon (New Living Translation): 1:1-4 "This is Solomon's song of songs, more wonderful than any other. Kiss me and kiss me again, for your love is sweeter than wine. How pleasing is your fragrance; your name is like the spreading fragrance of scented oils. No wonder all the young women love you! Take me with you; come, let's run! The king has brought me into his bedroom."

2:4-7: "He escorts me to the banquet hall; it's obvious how much he loves me. Strengthen me with raisin cakes, refresh me with apples, for I am weak with love His left arm is under my head, and his right arm embraces me. Promise me, O women of Jerusalem, by the gazelles and wild deer, not to awaken love until the time is right."

This is probably as good a time as any to state, *self-control* is a good attribute to practice. Just to be clear in what I'm referring to, I'm in no way referring to careless sexual behavior as the definition of passionate, romantic love. God is a god of covenant. His will for sexual relationships are to be within covenant.

If you have found the love of your life, you have received the most incredible and precious gift meant for a lifetime of pleasure, companionship, and love so deep it melds you together as one. I have observed and pondered in the depths of my heart this love so deep and powerful it brings two together as one. It grieves me to say, I have all too often experienced and witnessed it being overlooked or not tended to as the true treasure it is purposed to be. Too often, we allow pride, fear, complacency and many other walls of the heart to rob and cheat us from receiving and giving in full capacity. This love was intended to be a union of everything good and a completing (partnering) of one another to the best of our capabilities. Adam and Eve were originally placed together naked. That means they withheld nothing of themselves from one another. They were transparent without fear or shame in their relationship with one another. As one. It wasn't until their eyes were opened to the knowledge of good and evil that they become ashamed of their transparency/nakedness before one another. They, then hid themselves (by clothing themselves) from each other and from God.

Sin is missing the mark. When they became knowledgeable of good and evil, or in other words, of what perfectly hits the mark versus the shortcomings, then the focus of thought and perception, rather than simply being as one with another, became that of shame. Shame produced the loss of transparency and the fullness of surrender to one another, and *that* hindered their relationship. My point is, we are too often withholding it, when all the while we should be letting love abound and rule above all else. There is nothing more powerful, more valuable, more fulfilling, more sought after, more healing, or more eternal than love!

Someone once made a comment to me about a certain relationship being 'high maintenance'. If you know me at all you would know, the simplest of statements can and will most likely take me into a broader range of contemplation. As I pondered what might be considered *high maintenance*, I thought about the care we give to the vehicles we drive. Some vehicles truly are high maintenance and are continuously breaking down and in need of repair. Owning a vehicle automatically requires regular routine maintenance to keep it functioning as it should. Since we want to get the most out of our vehicle, we're willing without hesitation to do what is necessary to keep our vehicle functioning at its best. We regularly check the oil, fill it and change it as needed; we make sure it has enough fuel to take us where we need to go; we make sure the tires are properly balanced and rotated; we check to ensure there is the right amount of air in each tire; we wash the outside, clean the inside; check pressures and gauges and fluids, as well as a few other things, and we do this on a regular basis. Why? Because we know if we do not tend to these things the vehicle will not function at its best and possibly check out on us after a fleeting time span. Generally speaking, we've given a large amount of money for our vehicle and we want to keep it running smoothly for as long as possible. The things I mentioned aren't even considered to be high maintenance, merely regular routine maintenance. I was thinking, in comparison to the effort we put into maintaining a healthy relationship, how much are we willing to invest before we consider the relationship to be high maintenance. Shouldn't we be as willing or *more* willing to give regular care and attentiveness into a relationship? Obviously, there are certain attentiveness' needed to keep it functioning at its best, healthiest and with longevity, none of which are truly in the category of being high maintenance. Many are wanting to maintain relationships without fueling them up on a regular basis or checking the gauges and making the necessary adjustments. If our vehicle is worth it, why not see how much more valuable and rewarding it is to give effort, attention and intentional *TLC* into our relationships?

There are so many types of relationships; romantic, friendship, family – regardless of the type if we would allow – with intention – love to abound above all else, we would find we have all we've earnestly been searching after in our pursuit for happiness and success. When we can perceive love as it is meant to be perceived, we then are truly living life and passion in life and love would become alive and active within our hearts. There is no fear in perfect love (1 John 4:8), therefore, so many hindrances and walls in our relationships would melt away and we would experience freedoms and acceptance in being our transparent selves. We tend to complicate it much more than need be.

It's simply in deciding to love and receive love without conditions and negative perceptions. Why is it there's a glow to a person who is in love? Love breathes life into the depths of our beings. God is love (1 John 4:8). God is spirit (John 4:24). His spirit is life (John 10:10). When we love, and are loved (because we were created to love and be loved) it causes us to flourish and glow as if renewed with life from within. It's very much the same concept as, we were created to consume food to maintain good health. A healthy person in the natural, has a healthy appearance. A genuinely happy person, emits an appearance of being happy and likewise, a person who loves and receives loves, is healthy in their spiritual heart therefore their appearance testifies of it. We were designed to love and be loved just as much as we were designed to eat food for our health.

To love without conditions means we're not placing requirements and false expectations on other people and allowing that to determine whether we will issue love to them or not. We're to love at all times but keep in mind there are distinct levels and types of love as well as relationships. Love, genuine love without imposing conditions, gives the freedom for people to be themselves without fear of love being withheld. Also, when I refer to love without conditions, that doesn't mean having no boundaries in relationships. Loving without condition and having boundaries are two different topics. Destructive, abusive relationships are unacceptable. Safe, healthy boundaries are always to be implemented. If we love our children without condition, we love them regardless of what they do or how they behave. We don't lay down conditions for them by which they must earn our love. We simply love them. That's a fitting example of loving without conditions.

I'm a deep thinker. If you were to get to know me well that's one of the first things you'd probably discover out about me. I ponder pretty much everything! I will take a thought and turn it on every side that it possibly can be viewed from. My reasoning in doing that is to know exactly where my position is on whatever topic I happen to be pondering in that moment. I feel very prompted to give a little background of why I began to intentionally process and think deeply even about the small and insignificant topics. Being a person who contemplates the things in life seems to be a character trait sewn into the depths of who I am. Even so, there is a point of origin as to when I began to purposely do this in the extent that I do.

Many years ago, due to a series of circumstances and unhealthy relationships in my life, my self-worth became beaten down and without exaggeration; diminished. My mindset was as such; *I was born a person who was less-than everyone else and had nothing to say of which anyone would be interested in hearing,* therefore, with that mindset I didn't interject or contribute anything into conversation of my opinion whatsoever. After all, if it was my opinion it was most likely wrong and only annoying to those who would hear it. After hearing this told to me for years, I saw it as truth and formed the same belief about myself. So, I kept quiet.

Then it happened. One day while standing amongst a group of women discussing a heated topic, one woman looked at me and asked me what my thoughts were on the matter. I stood there dumb-founded, realizing I didn't have a clue. I had absolutely no idea as to what my opinion was either way. The sad truth was, not only had I stopped contributing anything to anyone else but I had also stopped allowing myself to have an opinion whatsoever. Basically, I had surrendered having an identity of my own due to such a low self-esteem. In my mind, I had no value and began to take a position as if having nothing of value to contribute. I hadn't realized I was to that point within myself until that very moment when someone inquired of me. Someone 'wanted' to know my thoughts and I had nothing to offer. The alarms were going off like crazy inside of me. *Whoop! Whoop! Whoop! Wake up Taffie!*

I was determined to not let that happen again. From that point on if no one else cared about what my opinion was, I wanted to know it - for myself. I felt if I were to have a specific stand on anything then I needed to know and understand myself very well. I wanted to know what provoked me to think as I did, so I began to ponder deeply. I began to search out my own heart and the root of every thought provoking me to think in whatever manner I did. Whatever the topic at hand was, I set out with intentions to search out; how it made me feel, why I felt the way the way I did about it, what was my foundation in what I believed, etc.? I decided God may know me inside and out better than I know myself, but I was going to be second in line to know and understand myself, as much as I possibly could.

So, I think deeply, I ponder, I process until I get my emotions, reactions, thoughts, origins of feelings and legitimacy of emotions (or lack of), figured out. Sometimes it takes only a few minutes and other times it's a lengthy process.

One time, I had a little fun with the idea of going out in public wearing my p.j.'s (similar to sweat pants) and no makeup on. On a social media site, I made a post about this little outing. In jest, I asked the local folks who might see me out at the store to pretend as if they didn't. The conversations which took place within the comments of my social media post prodded me to think a little deeper about the pressures of 'presentation' we place upon ourselves.

I had a friend who is single tell me what she's looking for in a potential mate. One of the things she listed was he would think she was perfect. As I pondered all the comments, opinions and my thoughts on this simple discussion of allowing myself to be seen in public looking 'not so good', I recalled her words spoken about wanting him to think of her as *perfect*. What exactly is 'perfect'?

In all truth and transparency of myself, most of the time if I go out it's with hair in place, makeup on and apparently from what I'm told, having a "put-together" look. One reason I do this is simply because it's something I really enjoy doing. I like fashion and makeup and I think it's fun. What can I say? I'm a girl!

If that's the only way you ever saw me, you might think that's the way I ALWAYS look. Trust me, it's not! In times past, I've had people who are *acquaintances* in my life tell me how I am *always* so 'put together' in my appearance. In their minds eye that's how I look as I go about my daily chores in my home. They formed an opinion of me that's not at all accurate. If they believe my appearance in public is my 'all the time' appearance, they're so mistaken. They would be highly disappointed when they saw me otherwise. If you came to my door at this very moment, you would be greeted by the me with; bedhead, no make-up, funky but oh-so-comfortable jogging pants - or 'lamb pants'. (Inside joke for when my friend, *Sally* - reads this!) and coffee on my breath! Put-together? Only in the sense that I'm not falling apart! My point is, if those people have expectations that I always have a specific appearance well, I'm sorry I can never live up to their expectations of me because it's not the reality of who I am.

When we say, "I love you", do we really mean; I love *you* when you look good and well-groomed? The *you* who is in decent shape, looking all put together? The *you* who only says the right thing at the right time? The *you* who is successful in your career? The *you* who is healthy? Is that what we mean by loving one another? Or do we mean, I love you - the *'you'* who is the heart of you- the very core and essence of who *you* really are?

Going back to my friend who wants to find a husband who sees her as perfect, I've thought about that in regard to the people who share a part of my life; family, friends, the love of my life - I don't want those who are truly in my life to think I'm perfect. That's an unrealistic image that I can NEVER live up to and would only explode into some zillion pieces if I tried, (or at least I would feel like it).

If they sincerely believed me to be perfect they would be so highly disappointed. By the way, I don't have anyone close to me who in any way, shape or form thinks I'm perfect. It doesn't take very long for them to see the truth behind that!

As insane as this sounds, don't we want the people who share a prominent place in our life to see us how we truly are? I do. I want them to see that I have junk and to understand what the junk is. Whether it be from the fact that I don't always look so great, to the extent that I have fears and struggles that I must work through. I want the people who are genuinely walking with me in life to love me for who I am - the whole kit and caboodle (the good, bad and the ugly) - not for who they want to believe I am. Please don't place me within the identity box you've formed of me when only having a small view of seeing me in all the perfect conditions. Nor for that fact, don't expect those whom you love to be perfect and place a false expectation upon them of which they cannot fulfill.

After all, isn't love about not having a blind eye to, or denying the flaws and issues we all have? Isn't it about seeing and knowing the flaws and issues, and then choosing to love and cover them? Isn't it about seeing there may be a smidgen of ugly, but a ton more of beauty; a smidgen of difficulties to work through but a ton more of delight to enjoy? Isn't it about having the ability to see the junk but not having your focus fixed upon it? There's so much more to us than the junk we're working through. The junk is such a small portion and can so easily be covered and viewed differently through the eyes of LOVE. As true as it is for the eyes of love to view us from a different angle, the eyes of love - real love - is not disillusioned. Love is perfectly capable of seeing the issues of people yet choosing to love beyond them. Even the most amazing, gifted and at-first-glance seemingly perfect people - are not perfect. They may seem like it at first but spend enough time with them and you'll see. We are ALL still in a process and that's 'perfectly' where we're supposed to be.

So, as far as a husband or family and friends who think I'm perfect, that's not for me. As for me, I want my peeps who walk through life with me to know I'm imperfect, and yet, love me anyway. I want the one who walks through life with me to love me when I'm ugly – when I have bedhead and bad breath, and to love me when I'm behaving ugly – knowing I'm not perfect but accepts me as the perfect one to walk through life with. Let me say, my husband upholds this role in my life very well. His example of unconditional love for me has been outstanding and humbling all in one.

Be accepting of who people are, generously love them as they are and be receptive to being accepted and loved exactly the way you are! We are perfectly, imperfect people. Receiving love without setting conditions upon ourselves is just as important. Oftentimes, we refuse to receive love from others because we don't view ourselves as being worthy just as we are. Therefore, we wall our heart from readily receiving love based on not having met our own measure of conditions.

Negative perceptions are what cause us to view the glass as half empty as opposed to half full. It causes the focus to be on what's lacking and flawed rather than focusing on what is available and good. If our perception is negative, our response and actions take on that negative form as well. If we would focus, praise and draw out what is positive, we would see people and our relationships flourish at a new level. Take for example, a plant that is properly cared for and given what is needed to thrive - it may begin with only a few branches and roots but after proper tending to, new sprouts develop bringing positive increase. It is now bearing what was already in existence plus the new growth.

Everything I've mentioned in our endeavor for happiness and success is nothing wrong, but then again, the happiness and contentment each hold is only temporary. Any of those endeavors being experienced with those whom you love become much sweeter. When you keep those who you love regarded as the most valuable and worthwhile pursuit, then all other endeavors become much more satisfying.

To love wholly is to live wholly!

"Love is patient and kind. Love is not jealous or boastful or proud or rude. It does not demand its own way. It is not irritable, and it keeps no record of being wronged. It does not rejoice about injustice but rejoices whenever the truth wins out. Love never gives up, never loses faith, is always hopeful, and endures through every circumstance. Prophecy and speaking in unknown languages and special knowledge will become useless. But love will last forever!" 1 Corinthians 13:48~NL Translation

CHAPTER 14

When Betrayal Knocks on Your Door

There's no questioning that we, as Believers have a very real enemy. If he can't have our spirit, he most certainly wants to rob us of anything and everything else he possibly can. He's cunning and often deceptively posing as something he's not. Here's the catch in that, with everything our enemy is, God is much more! Which means, for every plan and snare the enemy sets for us God has a plan already intact to stop us from stepping foot into the trap. If we do happen to find ourselves caught up in the enemy's trap, God has a plan for our release from it. It's all about whose voice we incline our hearing to and whom we choose to obey.

It all sounds easy enough, doesn't it? I mean honestly who would 'choose' to obey our enemy over our Father? That's the part where the enemy's cunningness comes into play. He tends to speak to our flesh, as to where God on the other hand, speaks to our spirit. The desires of our flesh can oftentimes become louder and temporarily more satisfying than the desires of our spirit man – or, at times we're momentarily deceived into believing so.

Have you ever been in a moment where the temptation of your flesh became so great that instead of doing or saying what you knew to be the right thing, you gave into your flesh for no other reason than because you wanted to? In the heat of the moment it felt good to let the flesh win the battle, didn't it? I'm not pleased to tell you, I have been there more than once. For the moment, it may have felt gratifying, then shortly afterwards there comes that small voice of wisdom whispering into your heart of hearts.

Possibly, the consequences of allowing the flesh to rule over the spirit began to appear one by one, declaring the mistake of a fleshly victory. The voice of conviction and the consequences, both have their unique way of shining the light of truth into the after-math of our decision-making skills. When void of self-control and Holy Spirit discernment the outcomes of our reactions speak rather loudly for themselves.

My point in saying all of this is, in all things God has a plan for our well-being and a plan that works out for our best in the outcome of the circumstance. The enemy can only have access to what we give him access to. Sure, he can try to get in and disrupt and may very well do so. His access in disrupting the flow of our Father's plans are only allowable on a temporary time table.

I equally like the translations from the *Amplified Bible* as well as *The Message* for 1 Peter 5:8-9 so I'm listing both shortly hereafter. As I study the word I often like to read the same scripture from several different translations and allow it to absorb into my understanding. The way one person phrases something differently from the way another person does can be the key to it clicking into the depth of our understanding. God speaks to each one of us in the manner and with the words we can best grasp as the individual person we are. With that being said, what a blessing it is to have different translations to study of the same word.

Amplified: "Be sober [well balanced and self-disciplined], be alert and cautious at all times. That enemy of yours, the devil, prowls around like a roaring lion [fiercely hungry], seeking someone to devour. But resist him, be firm in your faith [against his attack—rooted, established, immovable], knowing that the same experiences of suffering are being experienced by your brothers and sisters throughout the world." [You do not suffer alone.]

The Message: "Keep a cool head. Stay alert. The Devil is poised to pounce, and would like nothing better than to catch you napping. Keep your guard up. You're not the only ones plunged into these hard times. It's the same with Christians all over the world. So, keep a firm grip on the faith. The suffering won't last forever. It won't be long before this generous God who has great plans for us in Christ—eternal and glorious plans they are! —will have you put together and on your feet for good. He gets the last word; yes, he does."

We're at the very brink of so many promises, callings and opportunities of acceleration being at hand. It's an exciting time to experience on a personal level, as well as corporately. It's wisdom to keep in mind, (although not allowing it to become our priority of focus) during this time right at the brink of growth and expansion is when our enemy becomes the most determined to hinder our walk with the Lord. He will try to hinder us in our relationships with one another and in our success of advancement – personally and corporately. We need not be afraid, merely wise to his schemes and well prepared.

A while back, the Holy Spirit spoke a word to me about this very onslaught and tactic of the enemy upon my life personally. He has instructed me to share it with His people, that we all may be sharp and alert to the enemy's plans and prepared within our own hearts and minds. Recognizing the enemy at work is the greatest portion in winning the battle at hand. It's not unlike him to use the people we feel closest to. After all, that's where the greatest hurt and damage can be inflicted from when it's all said and done. We're all aware, the closer the relationship is the greater the wound of division from a relationship is. It's natural for our hearts to feel wounded and it's alright to feel the pain.

It's more of a matter of how we respond to the pain. When we respond by being led by the Spirit we do well, no matter how much pain we feel in the moment. The response from the flesh/emotions, which is more of a reaction than it is a response, is what causes the greatest disruption and chaotic consequences to enter our lives and to continue longer than what may have initially been averted.

"So, place yourselves under God's authority. Resist the devil, and he will run away from you." James 4:7
(GOD'S WORD Translation)

When we submit to God we are surrendering all we are to Him. Within us are emotions, words, and actions; all created by Him for submission to Him. Most importantly; keep in mind, in all that we do and say and feel, we are always His.

The Holy Spirit said to me, *"Tomorrow holds a clear and precise transition. There is a mantle coming upon My people – the mantle is falling. Let the sound of freedom ring. Freedom will be heard with a clear unmatched sound. There is danger up ahead, the enemy wants your head and is in hot pursuit to get it. Someone whom you have least expected will turn on you. Keep out of the snare by carefully choosing your words. Let each word be guided by My Spirit. I will disarm the plan and plot set out against you and remove the ammunition as you walk in obedience to My Spirit in every step of the way. Watch and pray. Be clean in every situation. This is a time where much prayer is required. The prayer will lift you above what is coming. What you have been waiting for will come as a result of this prayer feasting. Arise in the morning and begin with prayer. Let the prayer consume your day and end your waking hours with this continued prayer. Be filled. Be consumed. The days are numbered and none are to be spent in vain. The far-reaching impact of this fervent, hot prayer fast (feast) will far outweigh the time invested in it. You are a bona fide believer and it shall be known."*

If you're like me, I had never even used the word, 'bona fide', so I really wasn't sure what it meant exactly. In case you're in the same boat, the word *bona fide* from Merriam Webster's Dictionary - *'made of good faith without fraud or deceit; sincere; genuine.'*

Betrayal is a rough experience to go through regardless of the 'why's' or the 'how's' involved in it. Nevertheless, there's a side of it that we need to be mindful of but too often lose sight of because of the pain the betrayal itself inflicts upon us. The person whom we view as the betrayer, isn't necessarily setting out with evil or ill intent. There's a reason why satan is called a liar, a thief, an accuser of the brotherhood and desiring so much to divide the house of God. His schemes of attack are by lying to us about who we are, who our brothers and sisters are, and by trying to rob us of our authority and blessings we've been given. He accuses us not only to ourselves but also to one another and he wants to divide us to single us out into vulnerability.

"I'm sending you out like sheep among wolves. So be as cunning as snakes but as innocent as doves." Matthew 10:16 (GOD'S WORD Translation)

I believe it's safe to say, every one of us at some point in our lives has fallen prey to being deceived by the devil or having a part in believing an accusation about another member of the Body of Christ.

Just as we need grace personally for our sinful nature that still arises here and there, we also need to allow grace to be active on whoever may fall prey to that same deception against us. It's not easy, but it is doable through leaning on the Lord and following His instructions to us. It's called *forgiving*, and it comes by way of His active grace within our hearts. We don't know what avenue the enemy has accessed our fellow believers through. Take Peter for example, he betrayed Jesus, not because Peter was evil or meant harm to Jesus. He loved Jesus. Peter betrayed Jesus from the place of fear. Fear has a way of changing our perspective if we give it a place to roam around within us. Peter feared he would come under the same persecution as Jesus was, so he did what his fear was driving him to do and sought to protect his own well-being.

Just as the Father loved Jesus, He also loved Peter just as much. Just as the Father loves us, He loves the one who has sinned against us just as much. If He didn't love Peter as much as Jesus, (or any other sinner, which has us all covered in this discussion) He would not have sent His son to die for us all. Just as He has a plan for our advancement, He also has a plan for our betrayer's advancement too. We do well for our souls to pray for one another in every given situation.

We're all human and we all make mistakes. We sometimes make mistakes we wish we could take back and undo. Unfortunately, we cannot reverse time nor our actions. We can allow God's perfect grace to cover everything from our own sins to the sins of others within our life. His grace is more than sufficient to make new and good with all we have done wrong. Grace in action, in a sense is the reversal of time on our behalf, for our wrong decisions.

God is good!! He is loving and patient and takes our weaknesses, our trials and mistakes and creates something good from them. Have you noticed the areas we become best equipped to equip others in always seems to be our firsthand experiences where we've been the one in the *hot-seat?* He will bring us so much revelation and understanding in those experiences if we will seek Him and ask what it is He wants us to learn from them. When we have our 'on the mountaintop' experiences, we always come back down with fresh revelation. The same can be true for our 'valley' experiences as well, if you allow the Lord to bring it forth.

The word from the Lord I wrote about earlier in this chapter isn't really about the betrayer. When we are betrayed, in our vulnerability of the flesh it becomes tempting to focus on the betrayal itself. The word is more about the condition and preparation of our own heart in allowing His Spirit to rule over and above the voice of the enemy or above our own fleshly desire to react adversely when we're being wounded. The word is also about giving us a reminder of hope and reassurance of a good and rewarding outcome following our obedience through the trial.

God is a good Father and a good father prepares His children for good and bad situations. For those who mistakenly believe being a Believer of Christ means we will never endure hardships or trials, that's not true. God has clearly told us in His word while we're here on earth we'll go through some bad stuff. He also is faithful to instruct us how to walk through these times and always gives us the hope and promise of the reward to follow.

"I've told you this so that my peace will be with you. In the world, you'll have trouble. But cheer up! I have overcome the world."

John 16:33~God's Word Translation

Stretched for Expansion

Although not the most pleasurable topic, I'm going to talk about the aspect of sorrow in our tribulations. There's no way to get around it, in this world we're going to go through time of pain and trials.

"I have told you these things, so that in Me you may
have [perfect] peace. In the world you have
tribulation and distress and suffering, but be courageous [be
confident, be undaunted, be filled with joy]; I have overcome the
world." [My conquest is accomplished, My victory abiding.]
John 16:33 (Amplified Bible)

The Greek word for 'tribulation' is, *thlipsis, and* its definition is; *pressure, oppression, stress, anguish, tribulation, adversity, affliction, crushing, squashing, squeezing, distress.* I believe each and every one of us has at one time or another experienced seasons of these attributes of tribulation within our lives.

The amazing thing about the trials we face in life is that each one whether we realize it or not during the trial, holds the opportunity for us to be transformed. That transformation within our character can be one of becoming bitter and having a perspective of viewing life from an attitude of negativity. Or, we become empowered with a greater strength of overcoming and what we've so often referred to as an 'attitude of gratitude'. Whichever outcome of character we walk away with on the other side of the trial, whether you want to believe it or not, is all about what we as individuals have *chosen* to walk away with. *Perception is a choice.* We have a free will which entails our entire being; mind, heart and physical being. We choose to either focus on negativity or the positive, and whichever one we set our sights on is exactly what is absorbed into our core thus influencing our thoughts and actions to follow suit.

"Don't worry about anything; instead, pray about everything; tell God your needs, and don't forget to thank him for his answers. If you do this, you will experience God's peace, which is far more wonderful than the human mind can understand. His peace will keep your thoughts and your hearts quiet and at rest as you trust in Christ Jesus. And now, brothers, as I close this letter, let me say this one more thing: Fix your thoughts on what is true and good and right. Think about things that are pure and lovely, and dwell on the fine, good things in others. Think about all you can praise God for and be glad about." Philippians 4:6-8 (Living Bible)

In my lifetime, I have personally experienced several seasons of tribulation. None that I can say I would delight in walking through again. The positive side is, with every trial, I can say the lessons I learned and the awakening of truth within my heart I experienced as I walked through each one is as a priceless treasure to me. It's because of those times, I now know how to recognize and appreciate; life, love, grace, forgiveness, relationship, truth, blessing, joy, unity, passion, and the list continues to grow. If that doesn't make sense to you try thinking of it in this manner; if you have experienced the bondage of slavery, once you gain your freedom from slavery you can value and appreciate that freedom in a greater measure than the person who has never tasted the bondage of being enslaved.

"One of the Pharisees asked him over for a meal. He went to the Pharisee's house and sat down at the dinner table. Just then a woman of the village, the town harlot, having learned that Jesus was a guest in the home of the Pharisee, came with a bottle of very expensive perfume and stood at his feet, weeping, raining tears on his feet. Letting down her hair, she dried his feet, kissed them, and anointed them with the perfume. When the Pharisee who had invited him saw this, he said to himself, "If this man was the prophet I thought he was, he would have known what kind of woman this is who is falling all over him. Jesus said to him, "Simon, I have something to tell you. "Oh? Tell me." "Two men were in debt to a banker. One owed five hundred silver pieces, the other fifty. Neither of them could pay up, and so the banker canceled both debts. Which of the two would be more grateful?" Simon answered, "I suppose the one who was forgiven the most." "That's right," said Jesus. Then turning to the woman, but speaking to Simon, he said, "Do you see this woman? I came to your home; you provided no water for my feet, but she rained tears on my feet and dried them with her hair. You gave me no greeting, but from the time I arrived she hasn't quit kissing my feet. You provided nothing for freshening up, but she has soothed my feet with perfume. Impressive, isn't it? She was forgiven many, many sins, and so she is very, very grateful. If the forgiveness is minimal, the gratitude is minimal." Luke 7:36-47 (The Message)*

Several years ago, while at work, a co-worker and myself were lifting a large heavy object together when he lost his grip on it causing it to fall. I was able to get my hand minus one finger, out of the way of its landing spot. The impact of one-hundred and twenty pounds of metal landing on my one finger obviously broke it. There was some damage to the tissue, nerves and so on, which caused the appearance to be nasty as if some of it might be dying. As oddly as it sounds, one of the things the doctor looked for and found to be of hope for healing was although there was numbness, I could still feel pain when it was touched. His way of describing what was taking place within the nerves was, they were angry from the trauma but were still alive and wanting to heal up. As time passed, the pain lessened little by little as well as the numbness to sensations other than pain.

The point is, life happens and along its course there are unexpected events, some good that blesses our socks off and unfortunately, some that causes great pain. Even though we'd all prefer only the good, the bad happens too. Sometimes it's within the unpleasant events we learn how to appreciate the blessings even more. Did you know that once a broken bone has healed the scarring within it acts as a reinforcement and it becomes stronger than it was to begin with?

Interesting eh? So then, don't forget to count your blessings daily and to celebrate the good in life from the core of your heart of hearts. Allow the adverse events to impart the wisdom each experience has hidden within it and allow that wisdom to strengthen you. A sign of life isn't only found in the giggles, sometimes it's within the pain. Remember, if there's life there's hope too.

The key is to keep our eyes fixed upon Him and not the situation at hand. We're accountable for our own words and actions and it's important to remember to keep in continual communication, communion and surrender to the Lord. We're the children of a good Father and He has prepared for us a good testimony into the next chapter of our story.

Some years ago, the Lord brought my family and me from the state we had been born and raised in and relocated us into another beautiful state. Oregon. Prior to uprooting and relocating us He began to speak wonderful promises into our lives. He shared with us inspiring and hope filled words of what we could expect from this repositioning. From among the list, He told us of the joy we would have in the new homeland He was placing us into. He told us He was taking us into the new land as a part of our inheritance. Wow! Those are incredible promises in themselves let alone all the other powerful words He spoke prior to, during and after our move.

Just prior to the actual move, I began to have an incredibly strong draw in my spirit to another state as well. Sometimes it would become so intensely powerful that I would be confused between the two states of where exactly He wanted us to move to. So, I would inquire of Him over and over several times of exactly where He wanted us to be. He so patiently reconfirmed to me that indeed, it was Oregon but there was also something for a later time with the other state as well. Over the course of time, prophets and prophetic people began to speak to me about this other state. They began to speak of a relocation to this other state that would take place at a later date.

For the first year after we relocated it was wonderful. It was as if we had front row seats to witnessing the fulfillment of all the promises God had given us being made manifest in our lives! I was so extremely blessed and overflowing with joy for what the Lord was doing, almost daily I would have to restrain myself from crying tears of joy.

Then, what happened next felt like it came just as suddenly and as surprisingly as a blow to the head! Everything around me began to collapse and explode and just when I thought it couldn't possibly get any worse, it did. Have you ever watched one of those movies about a catastrophe hitting a city? The main actors and actresses are always in the center of the chaos and destruction and buildings are falling to the ground all around them. They barely escape from being crushed on the right and on the left. It seems like everywhere they look things are falling and blowing up! Will they make it out alive? Ok, a little dramatic effect but that's truly how it felt to me and to be transparent, the biggest buildings came down loud and hard, but the little ones kept crumbling around about me a little bit here and a little bit there for what seemed like the longest of time. Several years.

I would cry out, *'alright, what's up with this, God? This doesn't look like the land of my inheritance anymore. It looks more like the land of my destruction. What's up with that? Was I tricked? Was I misled? Did I misunderstand what You were saying when I thought you said move to Oregon? If you truly said to move here wouldn't it all be good and wonderful and I wouldn't be going through such chaos and destruction of so many different structures (so to speak) in my life?"* Those are the types of questions that tend to arise within us when things no longer seem to meet our expectations of how our promises should be brought into tangible existence. Any of those sound familiar to you?

Suddenly, almost EVERYTHING in my life appeared to be the opposite of all what I expected it to be and the opposite of what God told me it would be. God wants me to be forthright and transparent, exposing the thoughts of my heart, so, *that* I will do. I got to the point where a measure of doubt and discouragement began to intrude and when that happens, emotions begin to shout out to us. Perspective shifts into thinking these present circumstances are the way it will always be. The land I loved so dearly and saw as such a blessing and an answer to a long-time prayer had become a land I began to despise.

My focus changed to where I was no longer looking at the promises to emerge from the other side of my time of tribulation. The hidden victories taking place were nonexistent in my perspective. The only thing I could see for a while was everything falling and crumbling to the ground, to the right and to the left of me, nearly crushing me to pieces. I sincerely was not sure if I could withstand one more disappointment or hurt in my life. I had moments when I thought if anything else bad happens surely, I'm going to lose my sanity. Seriously, I wondered at times if I could emotionally handle anything else. Then, the next thing would happen and I survived it too wondering if I could possibly handle anything else. Then, yep, you got it, the next thing would happen and I survived. Then, the next and the next and the next.

Obviously, I have survived every trial that was sent my way, although some may argue if I kept my sanity intact. As much as I'd like to say to you I walked all of that out without wavering, I cannot say that. Shortly after the most intense heat of the explosions through all the discouragements and battle weariness, I decided the prophecies about the other state were looking pretty good to me. I wanted nothing more than to abort that season and all it carried for me and quickly move into the next season with all the great and wonderful promises it would hold. Sound good? Not good.

In every season of our life something is being tilled up, planted, weeds are being pulled up and the new is growing. New growth takes place even before we can see it happening. It begins underground or in other words, within the hidden place of the soul.

Let's use the example of a flower garden. Let's say we've had the same type of flowers and various plants in our garden for a while and desire to change its contents to having a fresh, new appearance. Before planting the new it's first necessary to remove the former bulbs from the ground, or else you'll end up with a mixture of the old and the new. We all know what must be done to get those bulbs out. It will require much digging into the ground. You'll need to go below the surface to get them, or when the new is sprouting forth the old will be springing up along with it. Of course, that result would not be the desired outcome if the garden was undergoing a transformation from the old garden to the new garden. We can liken this concept to what takes place beneath our surface during a time of transformation and the digging deep into our hearts and souls to remove the old roots. When it's time to remove what's been growing for a while and deeply rooted within us, there can be pain involved in the process. A portion of the pain might possibly be due to resistance in allowing the roots of familiarity to be pulled up and out. Painful but necessary to make room for the new to be planted and grown in purity void of the old stuff springing up with it. Ouch! If we abort the process without pulling up all the roots, part of the old continues to grow and our result is most likely having only a sparse garden, lacking its full potential. If we abort the process, giving up on planting the new, we merely have a barren and tilled up garden spot with nothing growing. If we continue through the pain of our labor making sure all the old is pulled up, the good ground tilled up and the new bulbs planted, at the time of full growth we then behold a beautiful garden filled with new life.

Enduring through the entirety can be a painful process but one that's necessary. When the fruit of its harvest springs up the process proves having been worthwhile confirmed through its beauty and fragrance. There's a priceless treasure to be found on the other side of enduring the tribulation, which is only for a time. The treasure is called, our *harvest*.

That time of trial for me appeared to be the total opposite of the promise of inheritance. The Lord gave me understanding, in the fulfillment of His promise to us the greatest blessings are also paralleled with some of the greatest warfare. When Jesus gained victory over the grave He first had to die, in the natural sense. He then, only after death to the natural self, overcame the grave for an everlasting victory.

"I can guarantee this truth: A single grain of wheat doesn't produce anything unless it is planted in the ground and dies. If it dies, it will produce a lot of grain." John 12:24
(GOD'S WORD Translation)

When the Lord took His people into the promised land the journey wasn't without battle. Nevertheless, He fully equipped them to overcome every battle and was preparing them all along the way to enter a land flowing with milk and honey. It was, without question *the* Promised Land and God was delighted with taking them into it. It was theirs. He was giving it to them. Did I mention there were giants dwelling there? Also, did you hear they had to first overcome the giants before they could take possession of the land?

"This was their report: "We arrived in the land you sent us to see, and it is indeed a magnificent country—a land 'flowing with milk and honey.' Here is some fruit we have brought as proof. But the people living there are powerful, and their cities are fortified and very large; and what's more, we saw Anakim giants there! The Amalekites live in the south, while in the hill country there are the Hittites, Jebusites, and Amorites; down along the coast of the Mediterranean Sea and in the Jordan River Valley are the Canaanites." But Caleb reassured the people as they stood before Moses. "Let us go up at once and possess it," he said, "for we are well able to conquer it!"
Numbers 13:27-30 (Living Bible)

"Then all the people began weeping aloud, and they carried on all night." (14:1)

"Why is the Lord bringing us to this land—just to have us die in battle? Our wives and children will be taken as prisoners of war! Wouldn't it be better for us to go back to Egypt?" 14:3 (GOD'S WORD Translation)

"At the same time, two of those who had explored the land, Joshua (son of Nun) and Caleb (son of Jephunneh), tore their clothes in despair. They said to the whole community of Israel, "The land we explored is very good. If the Lord is pleased with us, he will bring us into this land and give it to us. This is a land flowing with milk and honey! Don't rebel against the Lord, and don't be afraid of the people of the land. We will devour them like bread. They have no protection, and the Lord is with us. So, don't be afraid of them." 14:6-9

There will always be two choices of perspectives - the promise or the negative report. Focusing on the promise empowers us with the faith needed for receiving. Whereas, focusing on the negative report ensnares us with hopelessness and into our defeat. By faith in God's word (promises), we war when strong enough to and simply *stand* when unable to do anything other than that. I'd like to point out not all warfare is difficult, at times we warfare and not even realize that's what we're doing. At other times, we must be intentional about it. In my case, through a temporary wrong focus I was tempted to flee instead of stand and fight for the promises to be brought into completion. As I regained my perspective onto the original promise and words from God; hope, faith, strength and even love for where He's called me to be has returned with a greater appreciation. That's called overcoming.

Please don't misunderstand, I'm not tooting my own horn, it's a far cry from it. I quite humbly share this portion of my journey with you. I was nearly overcome because of a short but powerfully destructive and wrong perspective. God gets ALL the glory for every victory that through Him, we are made Overcomers!

"Finally, receive your power from the Lord and from his mighty strength. Put on all the armor that God supplies. In this way, you can take a stand against the devil's strategies. This is not a wrestling match against a human opponent. We are wrestling with rulers, authorities, the powers who govern this world of darkness, and spiritual forces that control evil in the heavenly world. For this reason, take up all the armor that God supplies. Then you will be able to take a stand during these evil days. Once you have overcome all obstacles, you will be able to stand your ground. So then, take your stand! Fasten truth around your waist like a belt. Put on God's approval as your breastplate. Put on your shoes so that you are ready to spread the Good News that gives peace. In addition to all these, take the Christian faith as your shield. With it you can put out all the flaming arrows of the evil one.   Also, take salvation as your helmet and God's word as the sword that the Spirit supplies. Pray in the Spirit in every situation. Use every kind of prayer and request there is. For the same reason, be alert. Use every kind of effort and make every kind of request for all of God's people." Ephesians 6:10-18
(GOD'S WORD Translation)

For much of us it's highly likely to say, we'd like to see expansion in our lives, in some if not all areas. Whether it'd be a pay increase, a job promotion, a bigger house, a larger sphere of influence, higher education, a bigger ministry or church, a more successful business, and this list could be never ending. What we oftentimes forget to consider is with increase into our lives also comes increased responsibilities and accountability.

"Jabez was a better man than his brothers, a man of honor. His mother had named him Jabez (Oh, the pain!), saying, "A painful birth! I bore him in great pain!" Jabez prayed to the God of Israel: "Bless me, O bless me! Give me land, large tracts of land. And provide your personal protection—don't let evil hurt me." God gave him what he asked." 1 Chronicles 4:10 (The Message)

"But someone who does not know, and then does something wrong, will be punished only lightly. When someone has been given much, much will be required in return; and when someone has been entrusted with much, even more will be required." Luke 12:48
(New Living Translation)

The idea of more sounds great and I'm not saying it's not. I believe it is, but often when we imagine increase being given to us we neglect to consider there will be a process of learning how to manage our newly instituted level of increase. When we find ourselves not transitioning as easily or as swiftly as what our mind's eye had imagined, we might tend to consider it as failure. Let me reassure you, what you might be tempted to view as failure, is not. It's the process of growth and with growth there are awkward stages and unpleasantness. Possibly even painful experiences. Growth is success. It's victory. It's conquering each step as it's presented, maybe not always at an all-out run but even a slow, steady pace is still growth.

"But don't begin until you count the cost. For who would begin construction of a building without first calculating the cost to see if there is enough money to finish it?" Luke 14:28 (NLT)

It's important we not be disillusioned with what it means to have more. Otherwise, it may set a tone for discouragement. There is no room for discouragement in our walk. Discouragement causes us to lose sight of truth and the promises we've been given by the Lord. Remember, He gave us more because He knows we can utilize it with success. Our responsibility is to not hold on too tight, instead, it's to continue to release it back to Him daily, allowing Him to teach and expand us. He believes in us and has equipped us with all we need to be victorious. Equipping us entails mostly of the process of uncovering the tools He's already allotted and distributed within us, and then discovering how to use them in the best and most successful manner.

We cannot have room for expansion in our lives without our lives' capacity being stretched. This is not always easy nor comfortable but always necessary and worth it.

Imagine your physical body stretching. We stretch our bodies to become more flexible and more able-bodied to perform better, knowing we will eventually master it with greater ease. A little bit of stretching feels good because it's within our comfort zone. It gets our endorphins flowing into our blood stream and that makes us feel a sense of life and energy charging through us. In fact, it kind of motivates us for movement similar to the way the thought of increase does to our brain.

On the other hand, when we want to increase our capacity of stretching beyond where we've been able to go, it may feel uncomfortable and even hurt somewhat. The pain is stimulated because we're going beyond the limits of where we've pushed ourselves prior to this. That's about the time we say *reality* sets in. When the natural realm becomes greater than our heavenly perspective, we claim that as reality. The natural is merely a temporary state and should not be comprehended as our so-called reality. The discomfort we experience in stretching our physical body, our spiritual person, or our stepping out of the comfort zone in whatever way it might be is only a temporary time of transition before we step into the greater reality of fulfilled promises from the Lord.

Think of it this way; stretching may hurt for a while but is creating more mobility and freedom of mobility in the long run. Within time, the benefits of stretching will outweigh the pain the body must endure at the onslaught and will little by little prove its productiveness. Time is the key word. In due time that which was once a struggle will become a piece of cake. One day, before we know it we'll realize all the stretching and pushing ourselves to go a little farther past our usual limit, all worked together to take us straight into our destiny. The seasons of stretching, with maybe even a little pain in the process, truly does carry a purpose and good fruit in the outcome.

The enemy's greatest and most strategic battlefield and oftentimes the most successful, takes place within the realm of our minds. If we can become discouraged, afraid, or lose our perspective of who we are in Him the enemy has won the battle – temporarily.

Losing our perspective usually takes place in times of continued discouragement or fear. When we lose our perspective of who *we* are, that's when we also begin to view others through the lens of being *less than* who they are. How we value ourselves is reflected in how we value those around us as well. Discouragement, fear and unworthiness are stemmed from deceptions of the enemy spoken into our thoughts. They come attempting to exaggerate the problem into appearing larger and more powerful than the promises of God. On the contrary, peace and joy are attributes of faith in God and His word.

The enemy of our soul wants nothing less than us to see ourselves as failures, outcasts, rejected, sick, poor, powerless, and unforgivable. Those are all lies to hinder us from the truth of who we really are. Our enemy doesn't always approach us in a way that is easily distinguishable of who he is. In fact, I believe it's safe to say, very rarely does he move in on us in an immediately recognizable manner. He's cunning, and therefore approaches us more-often-than-not in subtle ways that break down our faith, hope and self-confidence - over a habitual course of time rather than with one quick blow. These actions against us may come in a variety of forms that we least suspect is an avenue of the enemy, such as; a delayed time of breakthrough, a feeling of condemnation that we can't seem to shake, a critical word from a co-worker, or possibly with something so seemingly as innocent as a repeated struggle with getting a good night's sleep.

If we could grasp the truth of who we have been created to be, and the destiny we're meant to walk in we would be unstoppable for the kingdom of God and all the attacks of the enemy would be of no avail. *That*, my friend is the awesome truth!

We need to daily remind ourselves of this truth;

- ✓ God is my Father *(Matthew 23:9)* and in so being, He is my Healer *(Jehovah-Rapha; Exodus 15:26)*, my Provider *(Jehovah-Jireh): Genesis 22:14)*, my Restorer *(Jehovah-El Ashiyb: Psalm 23:3)*, my All in All *(Philippians 4:19)* because He provides unsparingly for His children *(Psalm 84:11)*. He IS a good and loving Father to me *(Psalm 136:1 and Jeremiah 31:3)*.

- ✓ He accepts me unconditionally, without fail – ALWAYS! (Ephesians 1:6)

- ✓ He ALWAYS wants my fellowship – yes, ALWAYS! (John 14:23)

- ✓ He has forgiven me – FOR EVERYTHING! (Isaiah 43:25-26)

- ✓ All that is His, He makes available to me. (Luke 12:32)

- ✓ He accepts me as I am, and yet as if I am already perfected. (2 Corinthians 5:17)

- ✓ HE receives me wholly as I am now, and yet gently guides and teaches me how to bear better and more productive fruit in my life. (John 15:16)

- ✓ Why? Because He wants the best of the best for me. Always! (Matthew 7:11 & Romans 8:28)

- ✓ God is for me – not against me. (Romans 8:31)

In His Word in one way or another, our Father has covered everything we could possibly need. He's declared to us promises and assurances, sufficient to cover all of life's trials and tribulations.

Be prepared to have those tent pegs moved farther out any day now. That's part of what the stretching season holds for you. Keep your eyes on the goal, knowing that any discomfort being felt is temporary and ultimately beneficial. The kingdom of God is limitless, therefore allow it to stretch you that you may have the muscle to carry more than what you are presently capable of.

"Listen carefully: I have given you
authority [that you now possess] to tread
on [a]serpents and scorpions, and [the
ability to exercise authority] over all the
power of the enemy (Satan); and nothing
will [in any way] harm you."

Luke 10:19~Amplified Bible

CHAPTER 16

The Kingdom is Here

For a period of about three to four days, every time I looked at the clock on my bathroom wall it was exactly one hour ahead. I noticed the time being off and reset it to the correct time. Then, the next time I went into the bathroom the time was off again! After several times of this pattern, I noticed not only was the time incorrect it was exactly one hour ahead, every time. I thought, *what in the world is with this clock?*

My bathroom has always been one of the places where I spend a lot of time in prayer and worship. If I put myself away into a prayer closet that's the one specific room I go to. It's the most private of any room in the house so it makes sense, right? In fact, I have spent so much time in the presence of the Lord in my bathroom, oftentimes I can just walk into it and immediately hear the voice of the Lord speaking insight and revelation to me. It makes sense to me that if the Lord were going to grab my attention by disrupting the time on a clock, it would be the clock in that room of the house. I can be slow on the draw about computing God is speaking to me through signs or repeated patterns of something. It took me somewhere in the timeframe of three to four days before it sank in, this was not a case of a malfunctioning clock. I mean after all, what clock malfunctions by moving the time ahead exactly one hour and then maintaining that time? The Lord wanted to speak something to me through this clock! When I finally 'got it' and asked the Lord what He wanted me to see in it, amid my state of delayed revelatory perception He said to me, *"The time of acceleration is at hand."* How ironic is that?! Obviously, the acceleration had not yet hit my prophetic gifting!

To clarify any misgivings of the possibility there may have indeed been a malfunction with the clock or the battery was dying, let me say this; once I recognized the Lord was speaking to me through the advancement of time with the clock, I then reset it one last time and it did not waver in keeping accurate time afterward. The way God chooses to speak to us is even creative. He is the Creator; therefore, He is always creative! Makes me excited to think about!

When John the Baptist and Jesus preached 'the kingdom of heaven is at hand', they weren't saying the kingdom of heaven is on its way or it's getting close, they were saying "it's here", "it's arrived". To say something is 'at hand' is to say, 'it's available now'.

To receive of something, you must be able to recognize the opportunity of availability of whatever that certain 'something' is. For this reason, being alert to the times and seasons and their impartations is highly crucial to the Body of Christ. The Lord has been speaking to us for a while about the acceleration coming. He has been preparing us to be knowledgeable, expectant and looking for it. Now He says it is here, it's upon us – the time of acceleration is now in the manifested state. He wants us to recognize its presence so that we may receive of it and walk in all of what He intends for it to bring us.

What does it mean for us if the time of acceleration is at hand? It means, the flood gates have opened and the 'suddenlies' are going to emerge – SUDDENLY! The 'suddenlies' are those promises and breakthroughs we have been waiting for.

The Holy Spirit said to me, *"The mighty hand of God is bringing the acceleration into your households and with it shall come the abundance, the deliverance and the intimate fellowship that has been the desire of your heart."*

Our loving Father certainly wants us to enjoy and rejoice in all He pours out upon us. It's good and right for us to celebrate Him for all His blessings. As parents, we take immense pleasure in seeing our children enjoy the gifts we bless them with. Our Father also delights in our enjoyment of His blessings to us.

Sometimes it can be easy to become caught up in the excitement and joy of the blessing and forget there remains a place of responsibility in stewardship. The last half of Luke 12:48 says, *"For everyone to whom much is given, from him much will be required; and to whom much has been committed, of him they will ask the more."* As each of us experience the floodgates of acceleration breaking through and being fulfilled in our lives, let's not forget our responsibility of stewardship in all the Father releases to us. We have a responsibility of stewardship stemming from the provision He supplies us with to that of being positioned into our destiny in the Lord. Not only will remembering the responsibility keep us motivated to properly handle with wisdom all that is given to us, it will allow our hearts to keep the Giver positioned above the gift.

"Now the company of believers was of one heart and soul, and not one [of them] claimed that anything belonging to him was [exclusively] his own, but everything was common property and for the use of all." Acts 4:32 (Amplified Bible)

Everything the Lord bestows upon us has a greater purpose than for us personally. Everything. As you can see in Acts, the early Church understood this well. They did not view what they had as being solely for themselves. They shared all they had possession of and because of their generosity with one another, they held nothing back and there was no lack among them.

"The evidence of the Spirit's presence is given to each person for the common good of everyone." 1 Corinthians 12:7
(GOD'S WORD Translation)

Not only does the Lord intend for us to share our material blessings with others He also instructs us to share every gift of the Holy Spirit as well. In Matthew 10:8 it is recorded that Jesus instructs His disciples in saying, *"Freely you have received, freely give."* The

Holy Spirit gave – not sold – each gift to us according to His will that all may benefit from its distribution. The profit of each gift is found only within the giving of it. For example, what profit is there in the gift of healing if one does not give it away to those in need of healing?

I recall early on in my days of prophesying publicly a time when I was feeling insecure with speaking upfront in church. The Lord had given me a word to share and I was silently arguing with Him about speaking it. I asked Him to instead tell the woman standing next to me because she a worship leader and was accustomed to being heard from the stage. Needless to say, I was politely scolded. It's what He spoke to me in the disciplinary words I want to share with you. They pierced me and I have never forgotten them, as they left quite the impact upon me. As I stood there requesting He send someone else to speak His words to the people, (sounds a bit like Moses, eh?) He said to me, *"I have not spoken these words to you for you to keep to yourself."* It wasn't about me. In fact, it wasn't about me or had nothing to do with me whatsoever, other than being the messenger for the Alpha and Omega, Himself. In other words, get over yourself Taffie, this is about something much bigger than your insecurities. I obeyed and although throughout the years I have still struggled from time to time with speaking publicly, I understand there's a bigger purpose than what I can see and I'm humbly grateful He allows me to have a purpose in delivering His messages to His people. He has commissioned me, *"As I tell it to you and teach it to you, you also tell it to and teach others."* The gift He has given to me isn't for me alone, it's divinely intended for sharing it with those He loves.

While I was just loving on the Lord in a sweet moment of worship, He spoke to me saying, *"There is now a releasing of three keys"*, and He then took me into a vision.

In the vision, I saw myself stepping from my kitchen into my dining room. I stood in the dining room looking down at my feet. I then saw Him lay a key on the floor in front of my feet. As I reached down to pick it up He said, ***"This one is wisdom."*** I began to take a step forward and then saw that on the floor in front of me was a door (in the floor). I bent down and inserted the key into the lock and opened it up. Inside was a type of storage area filled with what appeared to be clay pots or pitchers without handles. When I saw them my first thought was they were for me to fill up with water but as I began to scoop them up into my arms I had a vision within the vision and saw them being filled up with oil. After the pots were filled with oil I knew they were not for me only and I began to disperse them to many different people positioned a fair distance apart from one another. The Lord then said to me, *"This is to be used for reaching into many different regions."*

I then walked into the living room, and there was a second key placed directly into my hand. This key had the appearance of pure gold. It was beautiful. With the key in my left hand, I extended my arm up toward the ceiling and asked, *"What do I do with this one, Lord?"* He said, *"Place it in your mouth and taste how sweet the gold is on your tongue."* So, I placed it in my mouth and laid it upon my tongue. It tasted like honey melting into my mouth. He told me, *"This key opens mouths to speak My words from love."* I then saw myself kneeling on the floor with honey dripping from the corners of my mouth and I felt an overwhelming sense of peace and gratitude. A humbleness of spirit washed over me. I stayed knelt on my knees and silently worshiped from my heart because the Presence of the Lord was so great within the room. He said, *"This key is love. It speaks what I speak and it does what I do. This is the most valuable key of all, that is why it is gold."*

I stood up and immediately I saw a very bright light shining as if something was projecting light from within my eye. The light shone outwardly from my eye and was reflecting onto the front door of my house.

The third key was in my eye shining outwardly. I then heard the Father say to me, *"This key is in the eye of the beholder. It opens up vision to see from a higher perspective - from the kingdom view. It also will illuminate light for others that they may see farther ahead than they did without it."* As He spoke, the key in my eye began to glow brighter and brighter until it's light became so bright my natural eye was no longer visible - only the light that shone from it could be seen.

I then, walked out the front door of my house and He said to me, *"All of the keys I have given to you are not for you alone, they are all for sharing; for dispensing to others that which they unlock."* As I walked down the street I saw angels - ALLOT of angels! The angels were being sent out in all directions to assist people and some were on missions to interrupt assignments that people were still trying to accomplish but were from a past season and therefore no longer productive for this time and season. They were to oversee these people being moved onward, onto the present assignment of the present season. The vision ended there.

In this vision, I am not merely representing myself but also those within the Body of Christ who are true in heart and desiring to speak forth the 'good news of the gospel' in the original context. (The original context is love and GOOD news with no other agenda than salvation for all) The Good News has always been intended to be spoken from unconditional love and presented by way of actions (testifying of the Word). The oil signifies the presence of the Holy Spirit and provision. Both of which equip us with what is needed to be effectively reaching farther than what we can by our own accord. Words that are spoken from a heart of love (God is love); and as a light that shines through the darkness, reveal the Light (Jesus) to be seen rather than our own personal agendas of recognition.

As we humble ourselves before the Lord in a genuine heart of humility He will take us through a time of refining our lips to speak what is pure and true. There is so much depth to this golden key that it delivers me into such an awe of the Lord as I sense it within my spirit. The best way I can interpret what I feel in my spirit when watching this piece of the vision is, when our words are made pure and become His words we will enter a greater awareness of His goodness and therefore our words become a key to unlock the hearts of the hearers around us. This may be take place without our knowledge of it.

The rooms I saw myself in the vision have significance. The kitchen represents a place of preparation. The Lord told me earlier, *"The past several years have been a platform for you. A platform as a divine setup for what this year is about to bring into your life."*. We have been in a place of preparation for what we are about to step into.

A substantial number of the Body will be shifting from the place of preparing (kitchen) to the place of feasting and serving (dining room). It is in this place we will find what we didn't even realize we had stored away for such a time as this. The oil keeps us filled and overflows to others that they may be filled as well. (As the anointing and other provisions.) The first key given is wisdom. Wisdom is vital to know when and what to speak, where to go, who to speak to in the precise timing. Wisdom is, much needed discernment with strength of peace.

I moved to the living room to receive the next two keys. Just as the description of the room states, it is during our daily living, (our living space) in our homes, our workplaces, schools, wherever we may be spending our general day to day time is where we'll be speaking to others and shining the light from within us, for all to see Him.

Leaving through the front door is representative of implementing the keys He gave to us. There is an action of our faith being walked out so to speak, which also prompts the angelic hosts to begin their missions on our behalf.

This is a reestablishing of the foundation of who we are and the testimony coming forth from us - as His body of Believers being so powerful it cuts through all else and displays who Jesus is - in Truth, void of religion and all else that takes the form of godliness but is not.

He is seen! *He* is heard! And He is ensuring us to be in due season with what we are setting our focus upon.

Matthew 16:19 "And I will give you the keys of the Kingdom of Heaven; whatever doors you lock on earth shall be locked in heaven; and whatever doors you open on earth shall be open in heaven!" Matthew 16:19 (Living Bible)

Whether the Lord has blessed you with financial provision, a specific gifting, an anointing, deliverance, healing, with being solidly positioned into a calling, a talent, or even so much as a testimony - all have been given for the benefit of others. Wow! How awesome is the Lord and all His ways! It's so exciting to know when our Father thinks of one He is thinking of all and when HE blesses one His desire is to bless all!

The acceleration that is released into the life of one Believer is done so with the intentions that its good fruit will overflow into the lives of many! We are the Body. His Body. Each one, an extension of our Lord, all connected with Jesus as our Head. In Him we are loved and love. He is the life within our heart, enabling us into unity. All the pieces must connect to form a completion. He has given a piece to each one of us with His desire and admonition being; to freely give what we have been given. That is our blessings, wisdom, gifts, talents, possessions, and most importantly; LOVE.

'THE FLOODGATES HAVE OPENED; THE TIDAL WAVE HAS BEEN RELEASED. HAPPY SURFING!' says the Holy Spirit.

"God's kingdom isn't a matter of what you put in your stomach, for goodness' sake. It's what God does with your life as he sets it right, puts it together, and completes it with joy. Your task is to single-mindedly serve Christ. Do that and you'll kill two birds with one stone: pleasing the God above you and proving your worth to the people around you."

Romans 14:17-18~The Message

www.ingramcontent.com/pod-product-compliance
Lightning Source LLC
Chambersburg PA
CBHW072003060426
42446CB00042B/1573